RUNNING WITH JOY

RYAN HALL

HARVEST HOUSE PUBLISHERS

EUGENE, OREGON

Except where noted, Scripture quotations are from the New American Standard Bible®, © 1960, 1962, 1963, 1968, 1971, 1972, 1973, 1975, 1977, 1995 by The Lockman Foundation. Used by permission. (www.Lockman.org)

Verses marked NIV are from the Holy Bible, New International Version®, NIV®. Copyright © 1973, 1978, 1984 by Biblica, Inc.™ Used by permission of Zondervan. All rights reserved worldwide.

Verses marked NKJV are taken from the New King James Version. Copyright © 1982 by Thomas Nelson, Inc. Used by permission. All rights reserved.

Cover by Left Coast Design, Portland, Oregon

Cover photo © Victah Sailer

RUNNING WITH JOY
Copyright © 2011 by Ryan Hall
Published by Harvest House Publishers
Eugene, Oregon 97402
www.harvesthousepublishers.com

Library of Congress Cataloging-in-Publication Data
Hall, Ryan
Running with joy / Ryan Hall.
    p. cm.
ISBN 978-0-7369-4412-0 (pbk.)
1. Hall, Ryan 2. Long-distance runners—United States—Biography. I. Title.
GV1065.H24 2011
796.42092—dc22
[B]
                                                        2010031786

Printed in the United States of America

11 12 13 14 15 16 17 18 19 / LB-SK / 10 9 8 7 6 5 4 3 2 1

This book is dedicated
to my wife, Sara, and
to the many people
who have helped me find joy
regardless of whether
I win or lose.

INTRODUCTION

These things I have spoken to you so that My joy may
be in you, and that your joy may be made full.

JOHN 15:11

What we have seen and heard we proclaim to you also, so
that you too may have fellowship with us; and indeed our
fellowship is with the Father, and with His Son Jesus Christ.
These things we write, so that our joy may be made complete.

1 JOHN 1:3-4

I read these two verses and cannot help but smile. They capture the heart of what I want to share with you.

My journey as a runner began 14 years ago, at the age of 13, when I set out around Big Bear Lake for my first official run. The most recent chapter of my journey ended on Boylston Street at the end of the Boston Marathon on April 19, 2010, when I experienced complete, overflowing joy that had nothing to do with my performance. I've sought this joy my entire life as a runner but have rarely achieved it. Now, however, I believe that all people—athletes, businesspeople, parents, everyone—can have this joy regardless of what they do and how well they do it.

I had certainly experienced moments of joy before this and throughout my career, but they were almost always based on accomplishments, such as drastically improving my times, winning races, and setting records. All of these were tremendous experiences, but the problem was this: To experience joy, I had to win or set a record. If I didn't, joy was hard to find. I have been blessed with a very successful career, but I have also been a slave to performance. In fact, most of my athletic career at Stanford was a long, joyless dry spell.

Planting the Seeds

I used to hate to run—unless I was rounding the bases in baseball, hustling up and down the court in basketball, or returning kickoffs in football. Running just to run was the furthest thing from my mind until one life-changing day in the winter of my eighth-grade year. I was in a car, riding to a basketball game.

I have always been a dreamer. My siblings and I all played some kind of sport. My dad pitched for Pepperdine University and was drafted by the Baltimore Orioles. I wanted to follow in his footsteps—my dream was to be a pitcher in the major leagues, to one day stand out on the mound at Fenway Park—but as a five-foot tall middle schooler who barely tipped the scale into the triple digits, I spent most of my time sitting on the bench in basketball and football. I practiced pitching for hours in my backyard, usually throwing a tennis ball against the side of our house, inadvertently crushing all our Christmas lights in the process. Despite my work ethic, I struggled to get a fastball past my bigger and stronger peers.

In those days, my only athletic success seemed to be running the mile in PE. I broke the school record, running 5:32 as an eighth grader, but I didn't enjoy it. My dad was a triathlete and solid marathoner (around three hours), and he could see my God-given ability before I could. In fact, he told me I could be a world-class runner if I wanted. But I really wasn't interested in any sport that didn't have a ball—that is, until a normal car ride to a basketball game turned visionary.

I was 13, staring out the window of a Suburban full of rowdy, we-just-got-out-of-school-early teammates. But I wasn't feeling it. I was gazing out the window and daydreaming when I was suddenly overwhelmed with a crazy urge to run around the lake. The feeling is hard to describe—it was a vision from God, an unveiling, a seed He planted in me. In a moment, I could hardly wait to do something I would previously never have enjoyed. The desire was intense. (I experienced a similar moment years later when I first seriously considered moving up from the track to the marathon.)

The Saturday morning after that ride in the Suburban, I laced up my basketball shoes and headed out the door with my dad (who was curiously supportive of my bizarre idea) for what would prove to be a painful and slow 15-mile run around the lake. My hometown, Big Bear Lake, California, offers many cool things to do—skiing and snowboarding, skateboarding, fishing, baseball, basketball, football—but running was not among them. We had two dirt tracks (flooded with water most of the year) and no high-school track or cross-country teams. In those days, runners were seldom seen. I embarked on a journey that none of my peers could understand.

The run was hard—really hard. We had to make numerous stops, and by the time I finally walked through our front door and collapsed on the couch, morning had become afternoon. My calves ached like never before, my lungs burned from the thin air (we were running at 7000 feet), and I winced in pain with every step. My unorthodox shoe choice only made matters worse. I would never have imagined that such a painful first run would be the beginning of a running career. However, as I lay on the couch, my grumbling stomach begging for food, God planted two more seeds in me. One was that I had been given a gift to run with the best runners in the world. The other was that I could use that gift to help others. That epiphany launched my running journey.

Early Ups and Downs

By the time I graduated from high school, I had run 1500 meters in 3:42.7 (equivalent to a 4:00.5 mile and one of the fastest high-school 1500 meter times in America). I had picked up a national championship in the mile, a couple of state track and cross-country titles, and a scholarship to Stanford University, where I competed in cross-country and track for four years. Stanford had amazing facilities, faculty, teammates, coaches, and people…it was a great place to go to school. And best of all, it is where I met my wife to be, Sara.

However, my success in high-school running did not carry over into college. I struggled during my first three years and often felt like dropping out of school. In fact, I nearly quit during the winter of my sophomore year. I was fed up with working hard but never seeing my dreams come true, so I decided to take the winter quarter away from school. I headed home to get my life back to where I thought it needed to be if I was ever to run with the best runners in the world—something that seemed very unlikely at that point in my life. I was overweight, out of shape, discouraged, and battling bouts of depression.

Depression was a new experience for me. Growing up in a small town, I didn't have a lot of people to compete with, so I was somewhat successful in almost all of my endeavors. I was able to find satisfaction in what I did, and I learned to see myself as important because of my athletic achievements. When I went to college and began to struggle, finishing last place in race after race, I could no longer look at myself in the mirror and be happy with who I saw—an unsuccessful person, a failure, someone who was on a downward spiral. My poor running performance shook my view of who I was and what made me special. I struggled to maintain hope for the future.

When I went home, things initially got worse. Much worse. I became even more depressed and felt even further from realizing my dream. If Sara and my parents hadn't continued to encourage me, and especially if God hadn't given me that initial vision years earlier (which I was still clinging to), I probably would have given up.

One day during this rough period, my pastor asked me a helpful question: "What is the last thing you remember being certain that God wanted you to do?" I responded that when I was in high school, I was sure God wanted me to go to Stanford. But after struggling there for a year and half, Stanford didn't seem to be where I was supposed to be. Still, my pastor's comment reminded me that following God is not always easy or free from struggle, but it is the best way to live a full life. Once that was settled in my mind, I headed back to Stanford and committed myself to making the most of my time there and to finishing.

Marriage, Mammoth, and Marathons

Things didn't change right away, and I continued to struggle, but God encouraged me to keep running. I did have a few bright spots. I finished second in the 2003 NCAA Cross-Country Championships as a junior, which was a huge breakthrough for me, and our team won its second NCAA team title. In 2005, in an amazing three-week turn of events, I won the 2005 NCAA 5000-meter title, decided to turn pro, and proposed to Sara. I also qualified for the World Track and Field Championships—an honor equivalent to qualifying for the Olympics in an off year. Prior to my senior year, I had never even qualified for the NCAA Championships in track, and I hadn't been back to the U.S. qualifier meet for the World Championships since high school.

After failing to advance to the final at the World Championships, I returned to California, and Sara and I were married after a three-month engagement (six weeks of which were spent in Europe). Sara and I spent the next year living out of our car and training in Mammoth Lakes, California, with the talented Mammoth Track Club. I was finally starting to live my dream.

If anyone had asked me then if I would ever run a marathon as a professional, I would have said absolutely not. Even when Meb Keflezighi and Deena Kastor brought home medals for the U.S. in the 2004 Olympic Marathon (before we were teammates), I was not drawn to the distance and had no inkling I might be good at it. But at the 2006 U.S. Cross-Country Championships in New York, I had an experience much like my childhood vision of running around the lake.

I competed in the 4k championships (roughly 2.5 miles) and qualified for the World Cross-Country Championships to be held in Fokioka, Japan, a month or so later. My longer tempo runs had been very good leading up to the race, so I decided to come back the next day to run in the 12k championships. It's a rough double that isn't advised, especially with a stacked field.

The snow began falling in Van Cortland Park in the Bronx just prior to the gun. I would never have guessed what was about to transpire. Every once in a long while, runners have magical days when they run as effortlessly as if they were floating on clouds. This was my day, and the 12k was one of the easiest races I've ever run. Near the end of the race, in a moment of euphoria, I caught a glimpse of the sky, and at that instant, God planted a seed of curiosity in my heart. From that time on, I wondered what I could do at the longer distances. With the Olympics looming a little more than two years off, I was eager to find out.

On January 14, 2007, I found out why that seed was planted. In my first half-marathon, I ran an American record of 59:43 in another euphoric moment of ease. I felt as if I could have passed the finish line and run another half-marathon. This was the race that launched me into world-class running, opening the door for me to race that spring in perhaps the most competitive marathon in the world—the London Marathon.

Race day in London turned into a warm one, which would make the world record hard to beat, even for greats such as Haile Gebrselassie, Paul Tergat, Khalid Khannouchi, and Martin Lel. This was my first attempt at the rigorous 26.2-mile distance, so I planned to run in the second pack, which included the Olympic gold medalist Stefano Baldini, silver medalist (and later my teammate) Meb Keflezighi, and Marilson Gomes dos Santos of Brazil, who had recently been crowned the NYC Marathon champion. We ran the first half together, paced by a rabbit to run 2:07. But as we passed through the huge crowds at Tower Bridge at mile 13, I could no longer hold back. I took off after the lead and caught the greatest group of marathoners ever assembled. I ended up finishing seventh in an American debut record time of 2:08:24.

Since my debut, I have competed in six more marathons. In my second attempt, I won the 2008 U.S. Olympic Marathon Trials in a U.S. trials record of 2:09:02. Next, I went back to the London Marathon and finished fifth in 2:06:17 (a 4:48 per mile pace). It was the second-fastest marathon time ever run by an American.

The 2008 Olympic Marathon in Beijing called for my most challenging buildup and was my biggest learning experience. I reached the Bird's Nest (the National Stadium, where the race ends) in tenth place. This was initially a disappointment, but looking back on it now with wiser eyes, I see that it was exactly what I needed at that point in my career.

I rebounded nicely and finished third at the 2009 Boston Marathon. I was proud to be on the podium of a major marathon, and by fall of 2009, I felt it was my turn to win.

Do I Have What It Takes?

I went into the 2009 NYC Marathon in the best shape of my life, expecting to have an experience similar to the 2007 Houston half-marathon or the 2006 U.S. Cross-Country Championships in New York. That didn't happen. At 7 miles, a mysterious pain shot into my right hip that would remain to the finish. By 18 miles, a large lead pack had dropped me, and my time at 18 miles matched one I recorded in a training workout at 7000 feet on a much tougher course in the middle of a 140-mile week.

As I passed other fading runners and noticed guys who had dropped out of the race, I very much wanted to do the same. But my wife and I had just launched the Hall Steps Foundation. We had sponsored an at-risk school's running program in each of the five boroughs I was running through, and I had pledged my prize money to the foundation. The foundation was the fulfillment of the second part of my childhood vision—to use the gift God had given me to help others. Sara and I were amazed to see how running can change lives. We had the opportunity to work alongside Team World Vision the previous fall and meet the people who now had access to clean water because runners from around the country had raised money for wells. I'll never forget speaking with a man in his mid forties who told me that now, simply because his village had clean water, people there would live ten years longer. With this motivation fueling me, I rallied with everything I had over those very difficult last miles.

In retrospect, I probably used my best stuff in practice. I was able to manage a fourth-place finish in just over two hours and ten minutes, but I was very disappointed with my performance. As a professional athlete, I can easily get over races when I know going into them I'm not fit. But when I'm in the best shape of my life and still don't run well, disappointing performances are very hard to take. They make me question my mental, spiritual, and physical strength on that day. Do I have what it takes? If the answer is no, well, that can be very hard to handle.

It took me more than a few days or even weeks to process my experience in New York and move on. I had learned to carry around past disappointments for years without even knowing it. After New York, I knew this had to change. For more than a decade, I had endured an emotional roller coaster that was determined by my race results. I couldn't handle that anymore. I had to get free from my need to perform. I would achieve joy in my running regardless of the outcome, or I would get out. When I was younger, my dad often told me, "If it's not fun anymore, it's not worth doing it." Running wasn't fun anymore—not like this.

That brings me to January 9, 2010. It was a new year, and I was about to begin a new buildup. I had a little more than fourteen weeks until the 2010 Boston Marathon, and the disappointment of New York was about ten weeks behind me. With a fresh road ahead, I needed joy more than anything, win or lose. So that day, I decided to start keeping a journal. I felt the same sort of stirring that I felt in my spirit as a 13-year-old looking out over the lake. It was the same seed of excitement I felt when I looked into the sky during the U.S. 12k cross-country championships and knew I was going to become a marathoner. I was confident something special was waiting for me. But this time, it wouldn't be determined by my performance.

Before you start reading the journal, I should tell you a little about what my life is like when I'm not running—as well as some background behind the training regimen you'll see me endure day after day. I also want to tell you a bit about the Hall Steps Foundation, which is also part of the reason I decided to publish this book.

The Mammoth Track Club

During the time I wrote this journal, I did most of my training near my home in Mammoth Lakes, California. I have been blessed to travel the world, and I still feel that Mammoth is the most beautiful place on earth. It's located just south of Yosemite National Park, a little more than 300 miles north of Los Angeles. A big reason why I trained in Mammoth is the elevation—our home is at approximately 8000 feet. We can drive three miles in the summer and fall to train at 9000 feet or drive thirty miles in the winter to escape the snow and train at 4500 feet. The mountains are breathtaking and the forests are endless, with thousands of lakes, streams, and trails for summer adventure seekers to explore.

Summer is my favorite time of year here, but the gnarly winters can be long and difficult for runners who are training. Most of our trails are cross-country ski trails in winter, and we spent a lot of time in the car commuting to roads that were clear enough to run. The record annual snowfall is well over 50 feet, and the vast ski resort is often still in operation on July 4. Our home is like most others here. The living area is on the second floor because the first floor is often buried in snow.

THE MAMMOTH TRACK CLUB

Scott Bauhs	Dennis Kline
Josh Cox	Bob Larsen
Alistair Cragg	Terrence Mahon
Ryan Hall	Michael McKeeman
Sara Hall	Anna Pierce
Amy Hastings	Jonathan Pierce
Deena Kastor	Jen Rhines
Meb Keflezighi	Patrick Smythe
Rita Klabacha	Morgan Uceny

For five years, I trained with the elite Mammoth Track Club. It's a group of approximately a dozen runners with two coaches (Terrence Mahon and

Bob Larsen) and an assistant coach and exercise physiologist (Rita Klabacha). Sara, my wife, is also a professional runner, competing in 1500- and 5000-meter races. We met during our senior year in high school when we were both signing autographs. Sara noticed I wrote my favorite Bible verse at the time (Isaiah 40:31), got my e-mail address from a mutual friend, and e-mailed me. We both ended up at Stanford, where I had to act quickly because the guys at our preseason training camp in Mammoth were after her. We started dating the first week of our freshmen year, dated all four years, and were married three months after graduating. We both joined the team after our honeymoon to Costa Rica in the fall of 2005.

The team has included four 2008 Olympians including my former Stanford teammate Ian Dobson (5000 meters), Jen Rhines (5000 meters), Deena Kastor (2004 Olympic Marathon bronze medalist), and myself. Another teammate and close friend, Meb Keflezighi, failed to make the 2008 team due to injury, but he was the 2004 Olympic Marathon silver medalist. Sara ran valiantly and put herself in a position to make the 2008 team but finished just outside the top three. She is hoping to qualify for the 2012 games. Being married to a runner is a huge blessing. Few people can relate to the demands of training for a marathon, but my wife certainly can.

Our team was pivotal for my success. I needed Coach's expert training plan and feedback, and I also fed off—and, I hope, added to—the team's energy as we elevated each other's performance to new levels. However, in October 2010, Sara and I prayerfully decided to withdraw from the Mammoth Track Club. We are extremely grateful for all that our coach, teammates, and town have invested in us over the past five years, but the time has come for us to take the next step. We are looking forward to a more flexible training cycle.

Life as a Runner: Repeat, Repeat, and Repeat

The day-to-day life of a professional runner is not very glamorous. Whenever I feel like life has been pretty boring for the past couple of months, I know I am getting ready to run fast. Fortunately, I love the simple lifestyle. My personality and laid-back nature are perfect for being a professional runner. Still, sometimes I feel as if I'm living the movie *Groundhog Day*—new day, same routine.

A professional runner's lifestyle and a retiree's lifestyle are surprising similar. I often tell people I'm living my life in reverse. I get up, have breakfast and read my Bible, and go for a run at 8:30 (when all the seniors are out too). When I come back, I stretch and do some self-therapy on my legs. After lunch, I nap for an hour (two hours when I'm in a marathon buildup), go for another run (usually the shorter run of the day), and either do more self-therapy on my legs or go to the gym. (In my previous marathon build-ups, I was in the weight room for an hour a day, six days a week. But in this buildup, I spent more time doing other activities, such as self-therapy, to keep my legs loose.) After dinner, I have a couple of hours of free time and then usually go to bed between nine and ten. Repeat, repeat, and repeat.

In my free time I enjoy reading, fly fishing on occasion, watching movies with Sara, going to church, playing games with teammates, writing, playing with our two miniature Siberian huskies (Kai and Dash), and catching up on endless tasks to do around the house. Our team got together for dinner once every week or so, with the occasional party. We got along really well and enjoyed each other's company.

Sara and I are also love our church and are very active when we are in town. The Lighthouse is a nondenominational Christian church of 50 to 100 members that meets on Sunday evenings to accommodate the snowboarders who need to hit the fresh snow on Sunday mornings. Our church originated as a ministry to local snowboarders but now has outreaches in New Zealand, Canada, Switzerland, and Norway. It has a close working relationship with Bethel Church in Redding, California, though the churches are not directly affiliated.

Sara and I spend many hours watching ibethel.tv when both on the road and when doing self-therapy at home. Our faith has definitely grown in the past few years because of Bethel and the Lighthouse. One of the great things about our church is that it helps us build friendships outside of running. These relationships give balance to our lives in what would otherwise be an all-running, all-the-time world. Many of the members of the

Lighthouse are or were professional snowboarders, including Kelly Clark, the 2002 Olympic gold medalist and 2010 Olympic half-pipe bronze medalist. We learn a lot from their Christian–athletic perspective despite the differences in our sports.

Life is simple in the final four months before a marathon. The other months of the year, however, are more glamorous and filled with travel. I go to races to support Sara and to do appearances for my sponsors. My primary sponsor is Asics, but I also have working relationships or sponsorships with the Competitor Group (which puts on the Rock 'n' Roll marathon and half-marathon series around the country) and Nissan. Sara and I rarely race at the same event, which actually works out pretty well most of the time. Sara's peak seasons are in the winter and summer, and I peak in the spring and fall, except during an Olympic year, in which I also peak in the summer.

Coordinating our training and travel can be challenging. We both occasionally have to make sacrifices and train in places that are not necessarily ideal. Sara has been very supportive by enduring some brutally cold winters at altitude. Altitude training is very important for me if I expect to be competitive with world-class marathoners, almost all of whom train at high altitude in Africa.

A Little Extra Weight Goes a Long Way

Cooking becomes a point of interest for most professional runners because nutrition not only plays an obvious role in performance but also because it gives us something creative and fun to do together in the evenings. Sara is an excellent healthy chef. She even won a cooking contest at Stanford, so she is officially a pro. Our basic diet consists of lots of fresh veggies, whole grains and rice, organic meats (especially red meat for the iron), fruits, healthy fats, and of course, sweets (in moderation).

My nutrition has come a long way since my high-school days of eating a hot dog and ice cream minutes before heading out the door for a run. Now I try to eat many small meals throughout the day, making sure that I always have a little protein and healthy fat along with a coarse grain. I recently started working with nutritionist Dr. Clyde Wilson, a professor and advisor from Stanford, and have experienced an amazing shift in my energy sustainability throughout the day and in my weight management.

Weight is a bit of a touchy subject for distance runners. A couple pounds (too many or too few) can make a huge difference on race day. On the other hand, being too weight conscious is not helpful either. I never used to think about my weight when I was growing up. I just ate as much as I could as fast as I could. I was the middle of five kids in a family with limited resources, so I competed for food at the table. I remember hardly tasting it as I eyed my brothers' plates to see how much food they had left and how much was available for seconds. My active lifestyle kept me thin despite my competitive eating habits as a kid, but it wasn't enough to keep the weight off once I got to the buffet-style meals in the dorms at Stanford. I quickly went from 142 pounds to 150, which may not seem like a huge deal for a five-foot, ten-inch runner, but in a sport where being 1 percent on or off can make the difference between winning and not even qualifying, the extra eight pounds were detrimental to my running.

Even more detrimental were the patterns I developed once I became aware of the negative impact my weight had on my performance. By the end of my freshman year I was back down to my high-school weight, but I didn't get there in the proper way. Every day, I ate a peanut butter and jelly sandwich for breakfast, another one for lunch, and another for dinner. By the time I was at race weight, my body was zapped, and I was running worse than ever. My diet lacked energy and nutrients, and it wasn't sustainable. I quickly put back on the pounds after the discouraging end to my freshman year. I once took down a dozen Krispy Kreme donuts in a day. My weight fluctuated throughout college until I finally started to adjust to dorm life and developed healthier eating habits during my senior year.

Even so, my nutrition didn't become optimal until I began working with Dr. Clyde. Now I can enjoy some sweets and other foods I enjoy (I love cinnamon rolls) while also fueling my body with high-caliber, nutrient-dense foods. I race at a healthy 138 pounds, which my body has naturally come to after a prolonged period of fueling myself well while running the many training miles required to be in marathon shape. My nutritional advice is to enjoy putting high-caliber food into your body, treating your body well, and letting it find its proper weight for you based on your lifestyle. I always got myself into trouble when I started comparing my body to slightly built African runners. Now I just want to be the best version of me I can be, both inside and out.

Training: The Nitty-Gritty

Following the NYC Marathon, I took my customary two-week break from running, although because of my disappointment, I did a couple of crazy-hard mountain-bike rides during the second week. One was a steep three-hour climb from 7000 feet to 10,500 feet in my sandals. I hadn't intended to pull that off, but the view at the top restored my soul. I spent the next couple of weeks alternating an easy run one day with a mountain-bike ride the next, after which I returned to marathon training. During the couple of months preceding this journal, I focused on my shorter tempo runs. In essence, I was working on my 5k and 10k fitness.

I usually begin my true marathon-specific training 12 weeks before the marathon. For Boston, my buildup officially began on January 25, 2010, but I had been running hard for weeks prior. Coach usually gave us workouts in two-week cycles. His reasoning was simple: A body requires at least two weeks to respond to a workout and to become fitter for the next time the workout is repeated. For example, if I run a workout of eight miles at a five-minute pace, I wouldn't expect to be able to come back in one week and run much faster. But if I were to repeat the workout two weeks later, after completing workouts in the meantime that complemented my tempo fitness (such as intervals, sprints, and an uphill run), I would expect to be faster, assuming all other variables, such as wind, temperature, and elevation, are equal.

My workouts include several different types of runs.

1. *Warm-up and cooldown.* These runs are usually about three miles long and are at practically a jogging pace. We run them not to increase fitness but simply to prevent injuries.

2. *Easy runs.* During the difficult training for a marathon, my easy days are very slow (between seven and eight minutes per mile).

I usually run with the ladies, and we are very conversational the whole way. I include several easy runs each week.

3. *Intervals*. I usually do these workouts one day a week. The idea is to run several short, fast runs (at about 85 or 90 percent effort) with limited recovery time between them. By the end of the workout, I will usually have run a total of six miles, or about ten kilometers. Interval work is essential for increasing foot speed, developing 5k and 10k fitness, and making tempo runs not seem as fast.

4. *Tempo runs*. I do a tempo run once every week or two. If I could only do one workout a week to prepare for the marathon, it would be this. I run at the same pace (or at least the same effort) I hope to run in the marathon, but I obviously don't go as far. At the beginning of my buildup, my tempo runs are about four miles long. By the end of my buildup, they are between fifteen and eighteen miles. Tempo runs are important because they simulate the pace, effort, and mental challenges of a race.

5. *Long runs*. I usually do one long run every two weeks. Early in the buildup, long runs are about 13 miles. By two weeks prior to race day, I will have run several training runs longer than the marathon. During long runs, I try to run one minute per mile slower than marathon pace on a course similar to the marathon I am training for.

6. *Strides, sprints, and hill sprints*. These can be as short as 20 meters or as long as 300 meters. Sprints are all-out efforts, whereas I run strides at 90 to 95 percent effort. I run my hill sprints at maximum effort on grades that allow me to run about 75 percent as fast as I would be running on a flat course.

   Running sprints to prepare for a 26.2-mile race may seem counterintuitive, but it is essential for keeping up my leg speed during high-volume weeks. Here's the basic principle: Marathon fitness builds off half-marathon speed, which builds off 10k speed, which builds off 5k speed, which builds off mile speed, which builds off 400m speed, which builds off 100m speed. For example, right now, the difference between my mile fitness and my marathon fitness is roughly 45 seconds per mile. If I can get my mile fitness down another couple of seconds, perhaps my marathon speed will in turn drop another couple of seconds. That could mean the difference of a minute or more in a marathon, which is a huge amount of time in the world of elite running.

Now, it doesn't always work out this perfectly—if it did, the fastest milers in the world would also be the fastest marathoners. But Haile Gebrselassie, for instance, has run one of the fastest indoor 1500-meter times (3:31), yet he also holds the current marathon world record of 2:03:59.

When I run strides or sprints, I almost always also do drills—heel kicks, high knees, and so on—exercises that enhance my form and help me develop proper running mechanics and technique.

7. *Hill runs.* I usually do these on roads that steadily climb three to nine miles at a 5 to 7 percent grade. The effort level is about the same as a tempo run, but the pace is naturally much slower. Uphill runs build a lot of strength and are great for increasing fitness for both flat and hilly marathons. I usually find that my legs don't feel very tired the day after these runs, but I still get a great cardiovascular workout. After completing the run, I try to get a ride back down the hill because running downhill can wreak havoc on the legs.

8. *Marathon simulation.* This is the toughest workout I do. The distance can vary from 16 miles to 24 miles. I run the first half at the same effort as a long run (about a minute per mile slower than marathon pace). Then I change into my racing shoes and attempt to run the next half at marathon pace. I finish with a very short, slow cooldown. For example, I might run ten miles medium hard and ten miles hard with a two-mile cooldown.

Coach built these various runs into two-week cycles. This example is typical:

Week 1		
	Morning	**Afternoon**
Monday	Easy	Easy with sprints
Tuesday	Intervals	Easy
Wednesday	Medium-long run	Rest
Thursday	Easy	Easy with strides
Friday	Tempo run	Easy
Saturday	Easy	Easy
Sunday	Long run	Rest

Week 2		
	Morning	**Afternoon**
Monday	Easy or rest	Easy with sprints
Tuesday	Intervals	Easy
Wednesday	Easy	Easy
Thursday	Hill run	Easy with strides
Friday	Easy	Easy
Saturday	Marathon simulation	Rest
Sunday	Easy	Rest

The Hall Steps Foundation

In September of 2009, Sara and I launched the Hall Steps Foundation, urging the running community to join us as we take small steps toward the marathon goal of ending global poverty. The foundation's name comes from a quote from one of my inspirations, Mother Teresa: "I can do no great thing, just small things with great love." As in marathon training, the goal may seem distant and unreachable, but we can get there by focusing on the step right in front of us, taking each step one at a time with as much of our heart, mind, and spirit as we can muster. We formally launched the foundation less than a year ago, but it was born in my heart the day I collapsed on the couch after my first 15-mile run around the lake, when I caught the vision that God could use running to help others.

Of course, starting a foundation isn't the only way to help others. I want to encourage others by shaking their hands at expos; by including something in a blog post, tweet, or interview that motivates them; or simply by running in a way that inspires them. But more specifically, I have always had a heart for those who don't have the things they need. My family didn't have a lot of money growing up. Sometimes my mom complained when my dad trained for marathons because our grocery bill increased. We never went without a meal, but the experience made me empathize with those for whom hunger is a daily fact of life. And the Bible is filled with passages about loving and taking care of the needs of the poor, so as a Christian, doing nothing is not an option. In setting up the Hall Steps Foundation, I have learned that extreme poverty is actually a very solvable problem—multifaceted and complex, yes, but also fixable. We can do it, but only with a marathon effort and with many individuals doing many small and big things to help. I run nearly half a million steps while training for one marathon. Similarly, to defeat global poverty, we must all take many steps individually and then join with others who are running the race alongside us.

Sara too has always had a heart for the poor. While growing up, she often made trips from her home in Santa Rosa, California, down to San Francisco with bagged lunches for the homeless. She also took annual mission trips to Mexicali, Mexico, during the Easter week break. In college, she and I made similar trips together. She has always had a vision to serve impoverished communities in whatever way she can. She comes to life when she serves the poor. The decision to become a professional runner after college was difficult for her because of her strong desire to live among those in need. But we have both learned that right now, we can help best by using our gifts to run to the fullest. We launched the foundation so that all those who like to run, regardless of their ability level, and all those who simply want to do something healthy and challenging, can have community and a way to make an impact on the world.

To share what we have with those who are struggling is an honor and makes our lives richer in nonmaterial ways. I'm actually a little selfish—in a good way. I share my blessings, not because I feel obligated to or guilty if I don't, but partly because I experience the good life when I help others. People who build houses in Mexico for the homeless or work at soup kitchens in inner cities are always fired up and energized by the experience. Serving the poor is sometimes difficult, as is marathon training, but our efforts can make positive changes in people's lives, which will in turn effect changes in others, and so on and so on. Imagine such a world!

Our foundation allows anyone, anywhere, to run any race on behalf of the foundation to raise money, increase awareness, and perhaps help others smile because someone cares for them. To learn more about how to get involved in this radical movement of runners who are uniting to rid the world of poverty, check out our website at TheStepsFoundation.org. Just by buying this book, you have already contributed to helping the poor, because all royalties go to the Hall Steps Foundation.

Finding Joy

The journal entries that follow record my day-by-day journey to running with joy in any circumstances, including both in victory and in defeat. The words of the apostle Paul have taken on new meaning for me: "I have learned the secret of being content in any and every situation, whether well fed or hungry, whether living in plenty or in want. I can do everything through him who gives me strength."* Paul's secret is not that God can take him out of difficult situations, but rather that he can be content in the middle of them.

People often ask me about the message I want to bring to the running community and the world. My message is not that if you dream, live a focused life, and completely devote yourself to becoming the best runner in the world, it will happen. That message is simply not true. Or rather, it can only be true for one person at a time—the best runner in the world. Let me assure you, I would never want to discourage you from going after your goals with all your heart. I am all about going after whatever God has called you to do with everything in you. But my heart broke when I looked down the starting line at the Olympic games and realized that nearly all of us would be disappointed with our performance, because only three guys could make it on the podium.

---

* Philippians 4:12-13 NIV

But all of us, fast and slow alike, can experience something that is just as sweet as winning. My message is that even if you don't land on the podium or run a personal best, even if you have a bad workout or are struggling with an injury, you can experience joy to the fullest. I have been a slave for 14 years—a slave to my running times and race results. On April 19, 2010, I found freedom in the truth that joy is always available to us. The question is, will we let it in?

SATURDAY, JANUARY 9

Morning workout
▶ 20-minute warm-up with drills and strides
▶ 8-mile tempo run in 39:20
▶ 20-minute cooldown

Total miles: 13

Today's tempo run felt a lot better than the ten-mile tempo run two weeks ago. The weather was a lot warmer (mid thirties), and my legs had more pop in them even after a week of workouts. This time of year, 4:55 pace on Green Church Road at 7000 feet is a good, solid outing. My best is just under 4:50 pace. I felt controlled despite having Meb and Alistair sitting on my shoulder the whole way. I need to continue to get comfortable running in front.

I'm a little nervous about the half-marathon in Phoenix a week from tomorrow. I'm not sure what kind of time I should expect. I ran a six-mile tempo run at a 4:47 pace three weeks ago, but my ten miler two weeks ago was only 50:58 with a slow climb during the last two miles.

I reminded myself before the run that the only thing that matters is receiving Christ's love and giving it out to others. I think God wants to work on the way I see myself right now. Getting wrapped up in times and performances is so easy! Am I worthy of respect and love because of my fast pace during workouts and my race results, or am I an adopted child of God who is incredibly loved by the Creator of the universe simply because I am His child? Do I appreciate others for who they are, or do I judge them by their performance and value them only when they run well? These questions challenge me.

Yesterday afternoon, during my half-hour easy jog, I reflected on how easily I fall back into the mind-set I have struggled with in the past (and as recently as two months ago, just before the 2009 NYC Marathon), in which running becomes my entire world, an all-consuming obsession. God created me with a passionate, driven, and focused personality, but it can work against me when I focus more on the gift than on the God who lovingly gave me the gift.

Last Thursday, I ran a 40-minute hill run in the morning and then slugged through some intervals in the afternoon (8 by 200 in 32 seconds with a minute of rest in between), but I felt as flat as a pancake. It was a miserable day of running. But if I am happy and excited for life only when I'm running well, or if I begin to question God or get upset at Him after frustrating workouts, I know I've once again let running dictate my joy; I've become a slave to running. The apostle Paul calls it living according to the flesh, or the sinful nature. He makes clear that we should not walk in the flesh but in the Spirit.

When I walk in the Spirit, I am more alive and vibrant, and life is hopeful, beautiful, and exciting. When I see myself through God's eyes, I am secure and stable regardless of what is going on around me. But when I am looking at myself only through the eyes of a runner, I am constantly striving but on shaky ground, ready to collapse emotionally at the slightest physical injury. A runner's life is tiring and hard. It's a heavy load. I'm constantly trying to get faster and faster, and getting there is sweet, but then it's gone, and I spend the rest of my days trying to get back to that sweet spot—or past it to an even higher level. I'm tired of this constant striving.

In 2010, I'm focusing on the word *intimacy*. Intimacy with God—that's the goal of this year and of my life. When I am with Him, and when I see myself as He does, life is good even if I'm a bit overweight and out of shape. With Him, the mountaintops mean even more and are even sweeter, but with Him I also know that if I don't stay there, I will be okay.

Today Sara and I drove the four miles from our house to Mammoth

Mountain and watched the U.S. half-pipe Olympic qualifiers. I couldn't help but feel their freedom and joy. The riders went for it, each in his or her own way, all flying and going after the impossible. Shaun White quickly sealed his victory and a spot on the 2010 Olympic team on his first run, so he could enjoy his last run as a victory lap. He must have felt so free going into that final run. He had absolutely nothing to lose—he could ride simply for the pure joy of riding and show the rest of the world what is really lurking out there in the impossible. That can happen only when one is completely free of the pressure of having to perform well. I would love to do the same thing this year, competing with such freedom and joy that I am able to bring heaven down to earth. I believe the only way to do this is to be completely secure in who I am and totally full of God's love.

Last year, leading up to Boston 2009, I really wanted to bring heaven down to earth in my running and had been praying, *Your will be done on earth as it is in heaven.* But I had it backward. I was going after the impossible more than I was going after God. I was too interested in what God could do for me and not interested enough in simply receiving His love and being with Him. I recently heard a pastor say that the impossible flows out of intimacy with God. I'm going after that intimate relationship, not so I can do the impossible (although I would love to taste that!), but just because being with Him is the good life. I have a vision for how sweet life can be when we are caught up in His presence continually. In His arms, I sense a new freedom, a new awareness of His love. That's what I'm after.

Afternoon workout
▶ Easy 30-minute run
▶ Gym session

Total miles: 4

Felt decent but super tight at the gym. My quads are pulling on my patella quite a bit. My typical gym routine of core work, drills, and weights might not be the best considering my limited range of motion. I guess that's one result of years of marathon training. Lunges and step-ups are nearly impossible for me to do properly. I may have to step back from gym work for a while to get my legs loose enough to do the exercises correctly.

SUNDAY, JANUARY 10

Morning workout
▶ Easy 93-minute run

Total miles: 13

Legs felt a lot better than two weeks ago when I did this same medium-long run. It was nice to get out of the cold and drive the 30 miles down to Round Valley, where the dirt roads are clear for the entire winter. We make the 40-minute drive about three times a week during the winter months. Ran with Scotty, Amy, and Alistair. Deena, Meb, and Bryan* were not even in sight. They usually like to move along quicker than me on easy days. I have learned to be smart and listen to my body on my easy runs. Everyone has to find how they train best. In the afternoon, I took a two-hour nap, soaked in Epsom salts, and did some self-massage and stretching.

Right now I am trying to be flexible and allow God into more areas of my life. I have always been regimented in my diet, stretching routines, running routines, Bible reading, and so on. I like to set a schedule or routine and live by it. The carefully planned life has its place, but I don't want to be a slave to the schedule or feel like a failure if I don't stick to it. Falling off the schedule has sometimes been an enormous setback for me to overcome. I fixate on the schedule and focus on completing it rather than concentrating on what I am actually doing and living in the moment.

Similarly I'm currently following a program to read the Bible in a year, which is great, but often when I finish my daily reading, I can't remember anything I just read. My eyes are doing their job, but my heart isn't engaged. There is no point in reading the Bible—or stretching, or running, or whatever I may be doing—just to have done it. My heart must be fully present in my daily activities or they won't benefit me.

---

* Bryan lives part-time in Mammoth and is one of Meb's training partners.

FOURTEEN
WEEKS TO BOSTON

MONDAY, JANUARY 11

Morning workout
▶ Easy 60-minute run
Total miles: 8

Legs felt pretty good.

Afternoon workout
▶ 20-minute warm-up with drills
▶ 50-meter hill sprints, walk down, 50-meter flat sprint,
   3-minute rest—3 sets
▶ 10-minute cooldown
Total miles: 4

Legs felt okay.

TUESDAY, JANUARY 12

Morning workout
▶ 20-minute warm-up with drills
▶ Intervals: 4 by 1k with 2-minute rests. 4-minute rest, repeat
▶ 20-minute cooldown
Total miles: 11

Felt remarkably good. Despite the wind, I was still able to cut the interval times from 2:59 to 2:41. My speed on these Tuesday interval sessions is really starting to feel more comfortable. I think these workouts will be a big help for both my half-marathon and marathon. It was good to work out with Scotty and Josh. Scotty likes to race the last one, but I'm still learning how to run with the right amount of exertion. I let him go on the last one but was still running pretty much at full throttle. In hindsight, I probably should have relaxed a little more on the last one and finished feeling as if I could have run another mile if I needed to. Still learning.

TRAINING TO RACE VS. TRAINING TO GET FIT

What motivates you to run? As a professional runner, I train for months for a single race. You too may have a vision or goal—to complete a certain race, to improve your previous performance, or simply to get fit. On the other hand, you may train simply because you love to run and to exert yourself.

What is the best way to improve your fitness? Most beginners run the same time, distance, and effort every day. I strongly encourage you not to do this. Varying your pace, distance, and effort is not only more fun but also more effective. If you are bored with running, you might not be challenging yourself enough. If you're always tired and not improving, you might be pushing too hard every day.

I'm excited about what God is doing in me right now, and I'm feeling free because running isn't the most important thing in my life. Intimacy with God is so much sweeter than running fast. But ironically, as I get closer to God, apply His principles to my life more consistently, and allow the Holy Spirit to guide me more, I run better and enjoy my running more. I'm always tempted to feel as if I can use God to run faster, but I know this is shortchanging God's best for me. All I want is God. All I need is to receive His love. I need to continually ask myself, what is giving me joy today, my accomplishments or God's presence? "In Your presence is fullness of joy."* The key to joy is continually being in God's presence—running, working, eating, or even sleeping.

---

* Psalm 16:11

After all, what is it about winning or running fast that is so great? It's the *joy* that such an experience releases in us that makes us hungry for more. We were created to experience joy. The key to unlocking this daily, lasting, and more fulfilling joy isn't winning or setting personal bests—it's being with God as we run or do whatever we are doing. Sometimes our performance brings us joy, and we shouldn't feel guilty about enjoying those moments. Still, we must realize that we can't perform like that every day, but we can experience joy every day if we remain in God's presence.

Afternoon workout
▶ 35-minute run
Total miles: 5

Felt terrible today. My stomach was jacked. Not sure if it was from the vitamins, coffee, or tuna and shrimp I had for lunch. Probably it was a combination of vitamins (as I was burping them up) and the lunch. I need to go back to sandwiches for lunch. It's hard to pass up the tasty dinner leftovers, but I am over having painful afternoon runs as a result. Most of my afternoon runs have been terrible since I've been back in Mammoth and training hard. On my easy runs, I've had to work to keep Sara from dropping me, which doesn't do wonders for my confidence. I don't know, maybe it's running on the snow and slush that is killing me. Regardless, it's another opportunity to grow. I know that God has given me the keys to overcome challenges so I can become more like Him.

WEDNESDAY, JANUARY 13

Morning workout
▶ Easy 17-minute run
Total miles: 2

Started in six inches of fresh powder, and it was still dumping when I made a premature end to the run. Reminded me of my last run in Big Bear before the Houston Half-Marathon. I felt really good starting out today but had to stop the run because Sara wanted us to get to the airport early. I didn't have enough time to get in the full 85-minute run I'd planned, so I took the rest of the morning off before the flight to the Rock 'n' Roll Arizona Half-Marathon in Phoenix.

Afternoon workout
▶ 68-minute run

Total miles: 10

Legs felt like trash. Don't know what the deal is. So anticlimatic. Usually the first run down at sea level feels like a breeze, as if my feet weren't even touching the ground and I had a third lung. Not this time. Definitely my worst run ever at sea level considering I've just spent six weeks at altitude. My left knee flared up near the end of the run, which didn't help. I'm trying to keep a positive attitude, but it's tough. I want to see this as an opportunity for Christ to work in me and develop my character. Character training is harder than any workouts I do. Long day. Looking forward to some quiet time before the appearances start tomorrow.

THURSDAY, JANUARY 14

Morning workout
▶ 30-minute progression run (started slow and
     gradually accelerated to marathon pace)
▶ Drills
▶ Intervals: 8 by 200 meters at 32 seconds with 45-second rests
▶ 20-minute cooldown

Total miles: 9

Felt much better than yesterday. Have no idea what pace I was running because I forgot my Garmin. That may have been a blessing in disguise though. Better to go by feel at this point, being a couple days out from the race. Left knee was still tight. Felt good to have the sea-level effect I was missing yesterday. Nice to have Josh here because Sara went to Flagstaff to visit our former teammate and good friend Alicia Shay.

I know God is teaching me to see myself through His eyes. There is so much power in this. If I can just grasp the way God sees me, as someone who is accepted because of Jesus, everything will change, including a lot of foundational issues that drag me down. I long to sense the security I have in God's love. With that security I'm able to see everything else the way He does—not just running, but other people as well. I want to treat people the way He does, not in the way of the world. I long to have God's heart for the world. And that starts with seeing myself as He sees me.

Afternoon workout
▶ Easy 25-minute run
Total miles: 3.5

Felt a lot better than this morning.

HEART RATE MONITORS AND AEROBIC THRESHOLD

My heart rate monitor keeps me from running my uphill runs and tempo runs too hard. Simply watching my mile split times and paying attention to the way I feel works fine when everything is going according to plan, but when I'm working through sickness or running a new course, the heart rate monitor is much more effective. It also often reassures me that I am running hard enough on my tempo runs and long runs. When I check my watch and see a discouraging mile split (on the difficult uphill miles, for example), I check my heart rate and am assured that I am exerting the right amount of energy to get the most out of the workout.

If you go out too fast and struggle to run the last few miles of your long runs or tempo runs, use a heart rate monitor to keep your effort level under control in those early, easy miles.

What is the proper heart rate for your workouts? Begin by determining your maximum heart rate. If you have a fetish for pain, you can run as hard as you can and check your heart rate when you are near exhaustion, but I don't recommend that. As a starting point, subtract your age from 220. And remember, your maximum heart rate will go down not only as you get older but also as you get fitter.

When I am running easily, my target heart rate is 60 or 70 percent of my maximum heart rate. However, I rarely use a heart rate monitor on my easy days. Instead, I base my effort on how my legs are feeling simply because my heart rate doesn't always reflect my general energy level or leg fatigue. I want to run at a comfortable pace for my body for that day, and that varies from run to run.

On my tempo runs, I usually maintain about 170 beats per minute, or 88 percent of my maximum heart rate. On my longer tempo runs, my heart rate is closer to 165 in the first half and 170 in the second half. On my long runs, I try to keep my heart rate around 150 BPM, or 78 percent of my maximum heart rate.

If you are operating within 5 percent of these ranges and are able to maintain a consistent pace through the end of your workout, you have found your target heart rate for that particular run. Most beginners find that they are running much too hard on their easy runs and not hard enough on their hard days.

FRIDAY, JANUARY 15

Morning workout
▶ 40-minute run

Total miles: 6

Ran early before heading to the expo for a crazy day of media and appearances. Felt pretty sluggish. Yesterday I felt the positive effects of running at sea level, but I didn't today, which is weird. Missing the usual easiness that comes with the first week down. Not sure what is going on. Left knee is pretty sore.

SATURDAY, JANUARY 16

Morning workout
▶ Easy 35-minute run with drills and strides

Total miles: 5

Legs felt a little better than yesterday. Trying not to get worked up about tomorrow's race. I'm just not feeling super snappy, and my knee was really bothering me on my strides. I think it will all be fine. I just need God's perspective on things. The last couple of days before a race are always the toughest mentally.

Lots going on over the past couple of days with appearances. I really do enjoy connecting with people, although it is a little draining after a couple of hours just because it involves so much conversation. Being in race mode is difficult with so many appearances going on. My favorite appearance was running with the Kids Rock program at a school in the Phoenix area. We had a chance to speak and to run with third and fourth graders. I spoke about what it takes to be great in any endeavor and the need for resilience to get there. I said that failing is inevitable at some point in life, even for the most successful of people. Therefore, success doesn't mean never failing; it means getting back up. I urged the kids to always get up in life.

After the talk, we had a group run with the 200 high-energy youth. I was running with the kids when a young Hispanic boy passed me saying, "I win you!" Within a few strides he tripped over himself and tumbled onto the dry grass. I laughed out loud. Not long after, the boy ran his heart out to catch up to me and exclaimed, "I got back up." When I was talking to the kids, I thought most of them were in another world. I doubted they absorbed anything I said. Evidently I was wrong. It was great to feel like my time, words, and actions were touching lives.

SUNDAY, JANUARY 17

Morning workout

▶ 20-minute warm-up

▶ 13.1-mile race at Rock 'n' Roll Arizona Half-Marathon

▶ 20-minute cooldown

Total miles: 18

One of my roughest races of all time. Felt good on the warm-up. Incorporating a couple 30-second fast sprints in the warm-up made the early pace feel comfortable. Ran the first mile in 4:28, feeling like I was breathing pretty hard but feeling decent enough. It was exciting to go out hard because it has been a while since I have been on schedule to break my personal best for the half-marathon. I was thinking to myself that maybe I would have the race of my life and even run a world record. At the starting line, I always believe that anything is possible. However, a couple of miles later it was clear that this wouldn't be the day.

I kept a solid pace through two miles in 9 minutes flat before I began to slow. Passed through 10k in 29 minutes flat, which was the goal. I was going after an aggressive first 10k. I led the whole way through ten miles before lurking Simon Bairu made his move. I wasn't able to respond at all. My hip was hurting after four or five miles—the same sensation I had at NYC. Just didn't feel fluid at all. My left knee flared up about halfway, and my right foot was throbbing.

I contemplated stopping to loosen my shoelaces because of a shooting pain in my tendon on the top outside of my foot, but I decided I needed to push on. Felt like I was limping the whole last three miles. Glad to be done with this one. Definitely a long, painful race. Ended up running about 64 minutes but never cared to get my exact finishing time.

I made no physical breakthrough, but I was able to maintain a positive attitude throughout the race. I was thinking to myself the last mile that I needed to be gracious in both victory and defeat. I did my best to keep my head high afterward, but that was a challenge when talking to reporters, peers, family, friends, and spectators. I am learning to give myself more grace to not be perfect. I tend to be hard on myself, accepting nothing less than the spectacular. I am starting to see this as a lack of gratefulness. Also, I am learning that there is only so much I can do in my preparations. I certainly cannot force anything special to happen on the racecourse; I can only let out whatever energy is in me. Running is more art than science, and a few strokes can mean the difference between a mess and a masterpiece.

It was a very slow and painful cooldown. My left knee was really flared up, and I wondered if I might have broken my foot by running through the pain. Emotionally, the disappointment really set in on the cooldown. I knew that I went out too fast and just wasn't far enough along in my training to expect something special. That, coupled with physical pain, made for a long day. My disappointment really came from the feeling that I haven't had a really great day in a race for some time. My hope for the long term is running low.

I still believe with my whole heart that God has done amazing things in my running and have often been encouraged that He will continue to do so. For example, about eight weeks before the U.S. trials for the Olympic Marathon, I was in Mammoth training, and things were not going well. I was at the end of three days of depression and not running because of two weeks of steadily declining fitness for no apparent reason. I was working out the same as always, but something was wrong, and my body was not responding to the training the way it usually does. At the end of the three days, God began to pull me out of my despair, and I managed to make it to church that night. The speaker picked me out of the crowd and encouraged me with Psalm 20:5: "We will sing for joy over your victory, and in the name of our God we will set up our banners. May the LORD fulfill all your petitions."

I was at one of the lowest points in my career. Sara was in Europe at the time, and I remember telling her on the phone, "There is no way I'm going to make the team." I wasn't able to run a single mile at marathon pace. Things were not looking good, but I started training again and began feeling better. In the end, the Olympic trials race was one of the easiest wins I have ever had, but best of all was the connection I felt with God during the run.

When I returned to Big Bear, people had hung gigantic *banners* all around town with pictures of me pointing up to God at the end of the race. Our pastor's encouraging word was fulfilled literally.

Probably the most empowering comment I've ever received came from another speaker at our church, Stacey Campbell, last fall before the NYC Marathon. She reminded me of the story of Elijah, who was filled with the Spirit of God and outran a chariot to Jezreel. She spoke of supernatural running, which I was and continue to be so hungry to taste.

But believing what God can do is sometimes difficult when I'm not seeing it happen in my life. Still, faith is the substance of things unseen. I believe in God and in the promises He has given to me. I am holding on to those despite the way I am feeling at the moment. Regardless of how races go, God is still a good Papa who is always looking out for my best.

Week Two

THIRTEEN
WEEKS TO BOSTON

MONDAY, JANUARY 18

Morning workout
▶ Easy 70-minutes run

Total miles: 8.5

Ran some of the trails that surround Phoenix. My right foot is on fire, and my left knee is giving me problems. Fortunately, I got some great therapy yesterday, so things aren't as bad as I would expect after a day like yesterday. Got some ART* from Dr. John Ball. Then I saw big Andy, who does chiropractic adjustments and deep, deep, painful massage. Through these appointments I learned a lot about why I've been struggling recently, which is a total answer to prayer and welcome relief after yesterday's heavy spirit.

I learned that I have a lot of adhesions and scar tissue built up from years of hard training. The fact that I can't do squats, lunges, step-ups, or even bend down normally to pick something off the ground should have given me a hint that something was going on, but I have trained myself to ignore pain and tightness so I can push myself through discomfort. This is a great mentality in races but not the best for longevity. My legs are all gummed up, almost as if the muscles are glued together and need to be separated and cleared out. I've spent hours a day stretching and doing self-massage, and I even received 90 minutes of massage a day for the last ten weeks before NYC, but all that hasn't resulted in any relief from the pulling I'm feeling from my quads on the top of both of my patellas. Getting the right therapy is the key to unlocking the legs and getting back that youthful range of motion and fluidity that is the key to running.

---

* Active release technique, a type of massage therapy that focuses on separating muscles from each other and working out adhesions in the muscles.

I think this race will end up drastically altering my performance at the Boston Marathon because I am going to make proper therapy a priority and get my legs back to the way they were years ago.

Afternoon workout
▶ Easy 40-minute run

Total miles: 6.5

Wow. I feel a hundred times better than I did this morning. Today I had the most productive therapy session I have ever had. John watched me do a lunge and then worked mostly on my sciatic nerve, inner hamstring, hamstring, and quads for just a couple minutes. After that, I was able to do a lunge like I haven't been able to in years. My legs feel much more open and free. The muscles feel as if they've been unglued from each other, as if every muscle is now moving independently of the others, doing the job it was created to do. I still have a ways to go, but this was a massive improvement.

TUESDAY, JANUARY 19

Morning workout
▶ Easy 90-minute run

Total miles: 13.5

The last leg of our flight home yesterday was canceled due to snow, so we rented a car and tried to drive home from Reno. We picked up two stranded travelers who were trying to get to Mammoth as well (we had met one of them briefly). But the only road to Mammoth was closed halfway home, so we had to stop at a place with no vacancy in a small town. But a very kind, older lady felt compassion on Sara and me and our two fellow travelers, and we all shared the only room she had left.

When we got home, I ran in the snow. My legs felt much more open, and my knee isn't hurting near as badly. My foot is still really sore, but it just feels topical—nothing that affects the function of the foot. I just have to tie my shoe ridiculously loose. It's nice to have a rejuvenated sense of hope for the future. We're headed to my in-laws' house in Santa Rosa this evening to get a break from the Mammoth winter and to see a massage therapist who specializes in myofascial release. Glad to be getting out of Mammoth. Forecast is calling for ten feet of snow this week.

WEDNESDAY, JANUARY 20

Morning workout
▶ Easy 60-minute run with Sara

Total miles: 9

It's pouring rain here in Santa Rosa, but I don't mind because I'm so glad to run on roads and dirt trails instead of snow. Feels great to get out of altitude—I was ready for a break from the Mammoth winter. I should recover better and not feel so tired on my easy days. Later today, I'm supposed to see a great therapist named Jason Harman, who specializes in myofacial release. I hope he will be able to speed the recovery of my sore foot and knee.

Afternoon workout
▶ Easy 30-minute run with Sara

Total miles: 4

My legs feel a lot better after my first session with Jason. Myofascial release is difficult to describe—very artistic and holistic. Jason works so lightly that I can hardly tell something is actually happening, but other people have assured me that his work is effective. He is very tuned in to the body's energy, and he releases tension and adhesions that have been in the legs for years. I am excited about future treatments.

THURSDAY, JANUARY 21

Morning workout
▶ 20-minute warm-up
▶ 40-minute uphill run
▶ 10-minute cooldown

Total miles: 10

Okay, now I am sold on training in Santa Rosa. Loved the uphill Sara and I found off highway 12 (Trinity Road)—a small winding road with Italian writing painted on the road to encourage the riders who train there. It was a refreshing run for my spirit. I love to get in a low gear and just grind, working the hill on my own. I feel like Lance Armstrong looks when he is on one of his epic climbs. Love it.

It was pouring rain as I pounded up the hill with my Apple Nano blasting praise music in my ears. I felt very in control the whole time and could have pressed much harder. I want to end all my workouts feeling able to go farther. I want to leave something in the tank.

I've been considering a new training technique. I might take some time to adopt it, but I believe it's God's best plan for my body and spirit. At the beginning of 2010, God taught me that His kingdom comes with peace—a type of ease that results when you listen to the command that says, "Cease striving and know that I am God."* The peace of God's kingdom is released from God when we ask for it. We can't force it or earn it. So my primary goal is to receive the peace that comes from knowing God intimately and then to release that peace into everything I do. That peace gives me security and reminds me that as an adopted son of God, I don't have to prove my value or worth to myself or to the world. I am completely loved, accepted, and cherished by God. He is crazy about me, as He is with all those who accept His invitation to be with Him.

---

* Psalm 46:10

ALTERNATING FAST AND SLOW DAYS

Most runners run too easy on their fast days and too hard on their slow days. The basic principle of running is to break your muscles down on the workout days and then allow them to rebuild on the easy days. Take your easy days seriously and allow your body to recover. There is no point working the broken-down muscles again and again—your body will see little or no adaptation.

I used to hammer my workouts every day. I prided myself on being a hard worker and often competed with my teammates at Stanford when I should have been recovering with an easy run. My body could sustain such a training load for little while, but before we reached the championship portion of our season, I was tired and regressing rather than building fitness. I had a hard time understanding why I was working harder than everyone else and yet seeing the least amount of improvement.

When my pride finally gave way to frustration and I was forced to take my easy days seriously, I gradually began to improve. Now, having observed the best runners in the world, I realize that those with the most confidence run their easy runs the easiest. My coach at Stanford, Vin Lananna, used to say, "Where does the big elephant sit? Wherever it wants." Don't let others dictate your pace. Reject the need to compete and to prove yourself on every run. I do a lot of my easy runs with Sara and the other girls on our team because my body is telling me to take it easy.

Learn to pay attention to your body on easy days and hard days. No one else can feel what you are feeling or determine what is best for your body. When I am working out, I constantly ask myself, *Am I making a deposit today or a withdrawal?* Only you can answer that question.

When I run with this peace in my heart, I don't have to force workouts and races. I can relax and enjoy them, not feeling the need to prove anything to myself. I haven't been particularly good at implementing this methodology, but I'm confident that God has begun a work in me and will be faithful to complete it. He is unlocking His kingdom in my running. Jesus taught us to pray, "Your will be done, on earth as it is in heaven."* I don't want to force my training or racing; instead, I want to let the kingdom of God flow. My performance and results are not the keys to the kingdom. My sense of security comes from basking in God's love. I believe running with this secure, trusting, and joyful attitude will help me tap into God's tremendous power because that is how He created us to function.

Whenever I force my training to make special things happen, or I try to hit a home run in a workout or race, I usually end up with poor results. My best results have come when I wasn't expecting them. I hadn't thought about breaking the American record in the 2007 Houston Half-Marathon. I hadn't backed off my training at all and wasn't going into the race with the ambition of breaking an hour. The American record was set in the '80s and averaged 4:37 per mile, but when I came through the first mile in 4:37 and ended up averaging 4:33 per mile, I was completely shocked. Something came out of me that I didn't know was there. The race was a holy moment for me. It was one of the few times I have felt the Holy Spirit on me in a tangible way during a race.

Recently, God helped me better understand Luke 2:19: "Mary treasured all these things, pondering them in her heart." God appeared and revealed what was going to happen to and through her. When God reveals something He is going to do in your life, pondering these things in your heart is a powerful way to let God's vision for your life marinate in your soul and to release hope and joy for the future. It's almost like knowing you have a great poker hand but not wearing your emotions on your sleeve until the time comes to show your cards.

When I'm not secure in God's love, I pound my workouts as hard as I can. I have to show myself what I can do because I don't trust God to do something special. But now I'm learning to hold back and ponder what God is going to do in the race. My body responds best when I go to the well only on race day.

I feel less pressure during my workouts when I know I don't have to go to the well. I'm able to relax and enjoy the workout instead of feeling as if

---

* Matthew 6:10

I'm battling through every workout. At Stanford, Coach Lananna often asked us how we were feeling near the end of our workouts. If we said we were feeling good and wanted to run another repeat, he would normally reply, "Okay, you're done." If I leave something in the tank, my body will absorb training like a sponge. If I go to the tank time and time again, my body will continually get more and more tired. Taking it easy and not trying to prove myself on easy days requires self-control and security. But the rewards are great, and more importantly, the kingdom of God will flow.

Afternoon workout
▶ 20-minute warm-up
▶ Intervals: 6 by 300 meters (48 seconds each)
▶ 6 by 100 meters (15 seconds each)
▶ 1 by 200 meters (30 seconds)
▶ 10-minute cooldown

Total miles: 5.5

Felt so much better than two weeks ago. Despite the pouring rain and cooler temperatures, I felt a pop to my legs that has been missing for quite some time. Good day of running—with my legs coming around, workouts are a lot more fun. The change of atmosphere, training with Sara, and working out on my own is the winning formula for me to get my confidence back and get the snowball of positivity rolling. Back on the horse after a rough week!

FRIDAY, JANUARY 22

Morning workout
▶ Easy 60-minute run

Total miles: 8.5

Legs continue to feel better and better. The knee pain is almost gone, and the foot pain is getting a little better. Have more bounce in my step. Daily therapy is continuing to get the junk out and get my legs free and open.

Afternoon workout
▶ Easy 30-minute run

Total miles: 4

Felt pretty good. Feeling more and more like my old self. Excited for my tempo run on the infamous Sawyer Camp path tomorrow, just a ten-minute drive north of Stanford. We used to do some tempo runs there in college and in my first year as a pro. Sawyer Camp is a good place to gauge fitness. It is also where I first experienced a breakthrough in my tempo runs. My all-time best tempo run was eight miles at 4:35 per mile. I hope tomorrow holds something equally special.

SATURDAY, JANUARY 23

Morning workout
▶ 23-minute warm-up
▶ 8-mile tempo run
▶ 15-minute cooldown

Total miles: 13

Had a good one. I need to continue to work on running with confidence and security. Went out a little aggressively (4:39) and pushed the envelope a little too much. Averaged 4:40 pace through 3 miles and 4:47 pace for 8. Solid run. Legs felt much more fluid and open. It's good to know where I am at for the next time out, and a good place to be three months out. Just have to go three times as far.

Afternoon workout
▶ 35-minute run

Total miles: 5

Ran along Fisherman's Wharf in San Francisco. Legs still had some juice in them, which is exactly how I would like to leave them coming off all the workouts.

HILLS AND FLATS

I love to climb! Hill running is a great way to build strength and knee drive without zapping your body. Because of the low impact and slow speed, I can come back a few days after a hill run and do a hard long run. The hills provide many of the benefits I otherwise get in the gym, and I get a cardiovascular benefit as well. I have had some of my best races after doing substantial hill work. Here are two options you can try:

Uphill threshold. Run at the same effort as a tempo run for 30 minutes on a road with a grade you like. I enjoy a consistent 5 percent to 9 percent grade. If you're training for a marathon, gradually build up to 60 minutes. I never run back down because of the high impact of downhill running (unless I am training for a course like the Boston Marathon, which demands callusing to downhill running).

Hill sprints. Find a steep hill and sprint for 20 to 50 meters (10 repetitions). The key is to keep the distance short so you can sustain maximum effort with proper form.

SUNDAY, JANUARY 24

Morning workout
▶ Easy 2-hour run

Total miles: 18

Ran easy but at a decent clip in my old backyard—Huddart Park, where I did the majority of my long runs when I was at Stanford. Had a good run. During the first hour, I seemed to be holding something in my body— tension or stress or something. I thought it might have been stress from a phone call from Sara.

She told me the drug testers showed up at her parents' house because we forgot to update our location with our spontaneous overnight stay in San

Francisco after our Steps Foundation meeting and dinner last night. I already missed one test, and I have to report where I sleep every night and where the drug testers can easily reach me for an hour. All that can cause stressful moments, but I was holding something deeper in my spirit.*

About halfway through the run, as I headed up Lollipop Trail the second time, I realized I was carrying the same familiar burden. I was putting pressure on myself, just as I've done since childhood. When I played youth baseball, I put so much pressure on myself that I cried when I struck out. Now, I pressure myself to run fast, to win my next race, to prove to myself that I've got what it takes.

The truth is, I have "got it." But what I have was freely given to me and is freely given to all who want it. It's the gift of Jesus cleansing us once and for all, filling us with the Holy Spirit, and ushering us into heaven on earth and then ultimately into eternal life. What I have is so much better than winning Boston, but sometimes I lose sight of the most precious gift I have. It's as if I have a million dollars in the bank but don't remember it's there, so I spend my days begging on the streets to make ends meet.

As I was running, I realized I needed to totally release my burden, so that's what I did. I simply prayed, giving my emotional baggage to Jesus and asking Him to take it. I felt a lot lighter afterward and enjoyed the rest of my run and my day. I still want to win Boston, but I know that I have something sweeter than that in Jesus. Winning Boston would be an incredible opportunity and the realization of a lifelong dream, but I would be okay without it. Ironically, by letting go, I will be more able to grab hold of all that God has for me and my running.

---

* All professional runners must submit to drug testing. Missing three drug tests results in the same penalty as a positive drug test: a two-year ban from competing and a ban from the next Olympics.

TWELVE
WEEKS TO BOSTON

MONDAY, JANUARY 25

Morning workout
▶ 60-minute run

Total miles: 9

Ran in the rain. Felt pretty good. The therapy seems to be really taking hold, and I feel as if I am running much more fluidly, much more open. I'm finally relieved of many of the little aches and pains I have been experiencing for years. I'm glad we are getting in the therapy now.

Afternoon workout
▶ 30-minute warm-up with drills
▶ Sprints: 8 by 100 meters
▶ 6-minute cooldown

Total miles: 6

Legs felt pretty good. It's still raining, but I'll take rain over snow. My stomach was jacked up from an afternoon snack. I need to start eating simpler afternoon snacks. Healthy, wholesome snacks like I had this afternoon have their place, but so do easily digestible foods that may carry a few less vitamins, nutrients, and fiber but sit better in the stomach.

TUESDAY, JANUARY 26

Morning workout

▶ 20-minute warm-up with drills and strides
▶ I by 1200 meters with 3-minute rest
▶ 3 by I mile with 90-second rests
▶ I by 1200 meters
▶ 20-minute cooldown

Total miles: 11

Ran each 1200 in 3:18 and each mile in 4:33. I thought this workout was going to be a lot easier than it was. I guess that's how you know when you are about to be humbled. Whenever I expect a workout to be easy, I usually get my butt kicked. I have run similar times to these in Round Valley, but many of those were slightly downhill with training partners and on the road, which is slightly faster than the track. Today must have just been a slow day, because Sara didn't run as fast as she was hoping either. Some days are just slow for some reason. I am certainly getting better at handling them as I get older.

Dodging a high-school PE class didn't help, and the slight wind slowed us down a bit. I walked away from the workout with a better understanding of why I struggled so much with my half-marathon ten days ago and why I wasn't any faster at Sawyer camp last week on my tempo run. I am not fit enough to run in the 4:30 range for tempos yet. If I am doing intervals at low 4:30 pace, I shouldn't expect to run eight miles straight at 4:40 pace. I'm not many weeks away from doing that, but I'm expecting too much too early. My heart needs to trust completely in God and rest in Him, confident that He knows what's best for me. Today I choose to trust Him.

As I was finishing the workout, God planted the word *perspective* in my mind. I absolutely must keep the future in perspective and remember that today's workout is one step in a process. Even if I didn't run the workout at the level I wanted, it will help get me to finish Boston quicker than I otherwise could. I so easily get wrapped up in where I am at the moment and forget to look ahead to where I will be on April 19. God is encouraging me to be patient and to let my body come around.

SHORT AND LONG RUNS

To maximize your improvement throughout your training, find the proper balance of short recovery runs, workouts, and a weekly long run. Hitting the longer workouts and longer long runs seems to be more beneficial than running extra easy miles on the recovery days. I experimented with putting in two hours of running a day on my easy days leading up to Boston, but I eventually concluded that the excess easy running was leaving my legs flat going into workouts. I began to feel much better when I cut my easy running way down.

How far do long runs need to be? That depends on what you are training for. When I was training for 5k or 10k races, my long runs were not the emphasis of the week, and I usually ran two hours or less at a fairly easy pace. Now that I train for marathons and half-marathons, I run 26 miles a few times in my buildup at a moderately hard effort—but then I'm also trying to run a marathon under 2:10. I generally agree with the traditional model of a gradual ten-week buildup to a 20-mile run about a month before the marathon, followed by plenty of short, easy days.

Patience has always been difficult for God's people, including me. Once, when God gave a vision, He added, "It will certainly come, it will not delay."* A patient perspective allows me to roll with the good and the bad. When I lose a patient perspective, one bad workout can send me on a downward spiral very quickly. I cannot afford to lose hope or think negative thoughts.

Today I also remembered that a month after I set the half-marathon record in Arizona, running intervals at a 4:30 pace at sea level on the track didn't feel easy. In college, if I averaged 4:30s for our standard 6 by 1-mile workout, which we ran as our buildup for cross-country, I was ecstatic. I should

---

* Habakkuk 2:3

give myself more credit for today. Running is such a sport of momentum. I need to see every workout as good and beneficial (regardless of my pace) and build on the enthusiasm that comes with believing I am excelling over the long term.

On the cooldown I was talking with Sara about the difficult challenge of reaching my running goals, such as an hour for the half-marathon and 2:06 for the marathon. Having been at that level before, now I want to be there all the time, so I don't get excited about workouts that show I'm not back there yet. When I was first trying to get to break an hour in the half-marathon, I was thrilled with sub-five-minute pace on tempo runs on Green Church Road. Before long, I was able to run 4:55 pace, and the progress continued. But now I've run 4:48 pace on Green Church Road for 12 miles, so when I am recovering from a marathon or am not in particularly great shape, running 4:55 pace feels a whole lot less exciting than my best workouts did.

This is where the mental side of running comes into play in a huge way. Being okay with running slower than I have before and being patient enough to not force all my workouts to be at that same level is very challenging. I think this is why training is easier for me when I am bouncing around to new places. If I do a tempo run on a new course, I have nothing to compare it to, so I'm usually happy with the outcome and can usually improve on it as training progresses without overextending myself in workouts.

Afternoon workout
▶ Easy 45-minute run

Total miles: 6.5

Legs felt pretty good but my stomach was jacked again. I violated my own rule from yesterday after Sara brought in a tasty healthy Indian pumpkin tortilla thing from Whole Foods. Almost had to stop and throw it up. Not fun. Not again.

I was supposed to run only 25 minutes this afternoon, but I'm curious about trying out longer afternoon runs. I'm not sure if this is the Holy

Spirit's guidance, but it is something I have wanted to experiment with. I'll talk to Coach about this and see what he thinks. I think my legs might respond really well to a little more volume.

WEDNESDAY, JANUARY 27

Morning workout
▶ Easy 60-minute run

Total miles: 9

Legs felt a little tired this morning, maybe because of all the therapy, or maybe because of the workout. Took it easy.

Afternoon workout
▶ Easy 50-minute run
▶ Intervals: 8 by 200 meters in 30 seconds with 1-minute rests
▶ 5-minute cooldown

Total miles: 9

Legs felt okay—better once I did the intervals. I need to do more of them. They are the last thing I feel like doing when I am starting to run a little more, but they turn my legs on or get them firing. I am always glad after.

Stomach was jacked up again. Can't believe I did this to myself three days in a row. Sara helped me figure out the culprit—it was the salad I've been having for lunch. I made a salad yesterday at Whole Foods with all these dense and fibrous grains and veggies. I ate half yesterday and the rest today. But today I didn't have any vitamins and had a very simple snack, and I still had to stop and almost throw up from acid reflux. Good to get it figured out. I won't make that mistake again. Ouch!

THURSDAY, JANUARY 28

Morning workout
▶ Medium-long run (1 hour, 40 minutes)

Total miles: 14

Got up early to run before catching a flight to Miami to do some promo with Nissan at the Miami Marathon. A beautiful morning. Started the run in the dark and saw the sunrise through the mossy forest across the street from Sara's parents' house. It was one of those peaceful morning runs when everything feels perfect. Felt like I was getting a glimpse of heaven. God is so good.

Legs felt pretty good. Excited for the tempo run tomorrow in Miami. Meditated on this verse: "As he thinks in his heart, so is he."* Our minds are powerful tools God has given us. "If you have faith and do not doubt... even if you say to this mountain, 'Be taken up and cast into the sea,' it will happen."†

How do I see myself? Do I see myself as someone carrying the presence of God? Do I see myself the way God sees me? Do I envision myself as a world record holder in the marathon or a Boston Marathon champion? I confess that I don't always see myself the way I should—the way God sees me. God sees a man's heart because the heart determines the true value of a man. I often forget who I am—an adopted, redeemed, and freed child of God who carries the kingdom of God within me. As Jesus said, "The kingdom of God is within you."‡ It is so important that I pay attention to the way I see myself because it determines the way I look at every other aspect of my life. God, help me to see myself through Your lens.

---

* Proverbs 23:7 NKJV

† Matthew 21:21

‡ Luke 17:21 NIV

FRIDAY, JANUARY 29

Morning workout
▶ 20-minute warm-up
▶ 8-mile tempo run
▶ 20-minute cooldown
Total miles: 13.5

Today I gave myself a lot more credit for how well I ran in the 2008 Olympic Marathon. This morning was warm (mid seventies), humid, and windy for the tempo run. Can't believe it is winter here in Florida. I am like a melting snowman.

TRAINING AT ALTITUDE

Nearly all of the 2008 Beijing Olympians who won medals for races between 800 meters and the marathon utilized some altitude training.

I have lived at altitude since I was four years old. After months of hard marathon training, my first few days at sea level are almost euphoric. I call this the third-lung effect. Sara has to run with me to make sure I don't run too fast on my easy days.

Training at altitude was difficult for Sara her first few years, but now she seems to respond to it very well. I have found that the amount of altitude training I need varies from year to year. Try it sometime, even if only for a week's vacation, just to see if you too can experience the amazing third-lung effect.

Felt pretty flat today. Started off at what I thought would be a conservative pace (4:53 first mile and 4:47 second mile) but then had to slow down to run at the right effort level. It was a mental battle out there today. Running ten seconds per mile slower than last week doesn't make me feel like things are all going in the right direction, but I know that the travel, time change, and conditions took their toll on me.

I also think I didn't have adequate nutrition yesterday. Fuel is such an important part of marathon training. Making sure I get in adequate carbs when traveling and the day before the workout is very important. I had two small microwave burritos for lunch, a whole lot of veggies and fish for dinner, no snack at night, a bagel with cream cheese for breakfast, and no gel before the start. I think missing a few key carb choices during the previous 24 hours created an energy deficit that could account for the extra 1 or 2 percent that makes the difference between an okay tempo run and a great one. Today's tempo run was just okay.

The best part of the day was that God blessed me with some great new friends. A couple days ago, I received a random e-mail from a runner who offered to show me around Miami while I am here. I came down to the lobby not totally sure what to expect, but the people I met totally exceeded my expectations. Christian is a dedicated marathoner from Uruguay living in Miami and is part of a Latino running community here in Miami. I could tell just from the conversation in the car that these were special people.

They had two bikes to escort me along the best place to do a tempo run in Miami. The course is just steps from the water with no traffic lights to worry about. They gave me fluids, brought organic bananas for after the run, and took me to an organic healthy smoothie joint for recovery fuel, which was exactly what I was craving after melting in the heat. They wouldn't let me pay for tolls, food, or anything else and had nothing but encouragement for me after a somewhat disappointing workout.

Staying positive out there was difficult for me. After a couple of miles, when I was beginning to slow down, I really wasn't having much fun and couldn't help wanting the run to be over. After battling frustration for a couple of miles, I had to ease off the pedal so I could enjoy the run. When I know I am off, I have to take the edge off a bit—I can only do more damage by pushing harder.

Picturing myself winning Boston is difficult on days like this, but I am getting better at believing even when I am having an off day. I can still see it in my mind's eye, even when it's blurred by a trying day.

Afternoon workout
▶ Easy 30-minute run

Total miles: 4

Legs felt a little tired, but I enjoyed catching up with an old friend, Mike Sayenko (whom I got to know during a summer Christian running camp). Not too crazy at the marathon expo today. Met the famed Raven, who has run eight miles at four in the afternoon from his home in Miami for the past 20 years (even in hurricanes!). A character indeed. Black hair (head, face, and chest), black leather biker jacket…Seemed like a nice guy. Made me wonder if I need an image consultant.

SATURDAY, JANUARY 30

Morning workout
▶ Easy 60-minute run

Total miles: 9

Ran on a beautiful golf course that my new friends Christian and Omar took me too. Legs felt surprisingly good. Then we went to a raw, organic, vegan market that was off the hook. Possibly the best ice cream and tiramisu I have ever had.

Afternoon workout
▶ Easy 60-minute run with Sara

Total miles: 9

Weather was warm and humid, but I actually felt pretty good. The expo was buzzing today. So many marathoners, and so many of them knew all about the elites of the sport. I like the people in Miami. Ate dinner at Joe's Stone Crab with Nissan and Rodale sponsors. Amazing stone crab!

SUNDAY, JANUARY 31

Morning workout
▶ 2-hour progression run
Total miles: 19

Got up at 5:30 (ouch) to be the official starter of the Miami Marathon and then came back and slept for an hour. Went to the finish for an hour-long autograph signing at the Nissan booth and then came back and had a nut-butter sandwich, a muscle-milk protein shake, and some coffee. Started my run an hour later. Ran 55 minutes easy with Sara, 25 minutes at a medium pace (6:10 into the wind), and then ran 10 by 1 minute with 2 minutes of running easy. Ran 11.6 miles in 65 minutes for the second half. Felt really good coming back with the wind at my back. Had fun and felt fluid and more like my old self.

Afterward, Christian took Sara and me to the Turkish baths, which was really cool. They had a variety of hot and cold salt baths, steam rooms, sauna, hydrotherapy, and more. It was quite an experience. I have always wanted to do something like this. Then we went to a raw, organic, vegan "barbecue" with Christian and his other running teammates. (They call it a barbecue, but all the cooking is done at extremely low temperature to avoid killing the nutrients.) I had a great time connecting with their group. Sara and I wished we could spend more time with them.

Week Four

ELEVEN
WEEKS TO BOSTON

MONDAY, FEBRUARY I

Morning workout
▶ Easy 75-minute run
Total miles: 10

Felt a little tired today, but I guess that is to be expected. Ran the whole thing on grass fields surrounding a track while Sara was working out.

Afternoon workout
▶ Easy 45-minute run
Total miles: 6

Traveled to Boston to start a weeklong training stint on the marathon course and to watch Sara race indoors on Saturday. Felt really good on my run. Ran the last three miles or so of the course out and back. It's cold here in Boston, especially after being in Miami.

Feeling tired this morning but good this afternoon makes me wonder about the mental and emotional components of running and their impact on the physical. I felt pretty tired just six hours ago, but with the excitement and joy of being on the Boston Marathon course, I am suddenly feeling like a million bucks. There is definitely an emotional-physical connection to running.

The Holy Spirit is helping me understand the way a negative or unenthusiastic mind-set makes me feel more fatigued physically. I am having trouble figuring out how to maintain momentum when workouts are not great. Reversing the negative snowball effect of bad workouts is difficult, but the key surely includes guarding my heart and not letting the negative thoughts grow. Those thoughts will come, but I must nip them in the bud. If I dwell on them, the result can be that downward spiral I've suffered so many times in my athletic career. The good news is that positive thoughts can create the opposite effect just as powerfully and enhance my physical performance. Negative thoughts are runners' biggest enemy.

TUESDAY, FEBRUARY 2

Morning workout
- ▶ 20-minute warm-up run with drills and strides
- ▶ Intervals: 2k (4:37 pace) with 4-minute jog
- ▶ 4 by 1 mile at 4:50 pace with 75-second jog
- ▶ 4-minute rest
- ▶ 2k (4:33 pace)
- ▶ 20-minute cooldown

Total miles: 14

Ran from Hopkington to just past Wellesley.* Enjoyed seeing the course and felt some pop in my legs. The course is tougher than I remember. Seems to always be going up and down. Still, I love training on the course and getting familiar with it, which will certainly pay off on race day. Had fun out there, which is what it all comes down to.

I know how I want to run this marathon and how I want to come out the door for every training run. God has given me a vision of living with overflowing joy. Just loving the simple act of running and doing what I was created to do in close connection with God—running only because my Papa smiles when He watches me run. Running with this joy is all I want to do.

Afternoon workout
- ▶ Easy 45-minute run

Total miles: 6

Felt good. Having fun in Boston!

---

* Hopkington is the small town where the Boston Marathon begins, and Wellesley is the halfway point.

TRAILS, TRACKS, AND PAVEMENT

I try to match a running surface (trails, a track, or pavement) with the nature of a run. If I am recovering from a hard workout or a slight injury, I try to stay on soft surfaces.

We don't have a track yet in Mammoth (my teammate Deena is working on that), but if we did, I would certainly utilize it for interval and sprint workouts. Even though I'm training for a road race, a track can help me draw out that bit of extra speed during sprints.

All the rest of my hard running is on pavement. I need to callus my legs to the pounding of the pavement, especially for races like the Boston Marathon that really punish the legs with a series of downhills. The only way to prepare for the pavement is to practice on the pavement.

WEDNESDAY, FEBRUARY 3

Morning workout
▶ Easy 75-minute run

Total miles: 11

Ran out and back on the last five miles of the course. A little snowy this morning, but I still had fun checking out the course. Getting pretty familiar with the last five miles. Legs felt a little tired on the way out, but they felt better on the way back. Funny how that works.

Afternoon workout
▶ Easy 45-minute run

Total miles: 6

Legs felt pretty good.

THURSDAY, FEBRUARY 4

Morning workout
▶ 20-minute warm-up
▶ Medium 60-minute fartlek* run
▶ 20-minute cooldown

Total miles: 14

Started at the fire station (17.5 mile mark in the marathon), ran up and over the three hills in Newton (including the infamous Heartbreak Hill), and ended about half a mile down the graveyard mile (about 21.5 mile mark), where a car took me back down the hill to the fire station so I could run the four miles again. Love this workout. Felt really good. Goal was to work the hills hard and then float the recovery sections. Ran two minutes faster the second time around this demanding four-mile stretch without any extra effort. Shows the advantage of knowing the course. Ran nearly five-minute pace in my DS Trainers on the second round. Not bad for not even having my racing flats on. I am very pleased with the workout.

I am starting to think about coming to Boston earlier than my usual four or five days before the marathon, perhaps even as much as eight weeks early. I've always been adamant about spending my entire marathon buildup at altitude, but now I am now more open to sea-level training, so I figure if I am going to be at sea level, I might as well be on the Boston course. Bill Rodgers, Joan Benoit Samuelson, Greg Meyer, and others who ran well in the Boston Marathon trained and lived in Boston and knew this course like the back of their hands. Now that I have seen the benefit of knowing even just this technical four-mile stretch, I feel strongly in my spirit that I should train here. My soul feels at peace here. I love the course and the enthusiastic runners in the Boston area.

Afternoon workout
▶ Easy 40-minute run

Total miles: 5.5

Felt good. Legs keep feeling better and better. Going to see a therapist

---

* A free-flowing run with alternating faster and slower sections.

tonight to see if I can continue to get my glut med sorted out.* Eight miles into last year's NYC Marathon, I had a shooting pain in my right hip. It was a weird tightness that I'd never felt before in training or previous races that suddenly felt like it might take me out of the race, though I was able to work through it and still run reasonably well. After a two-week break, it was still not better and has bothered me to a small extent in training ever since. I don't want to have the same problem in the Boston Marathon. Massage, ART, stretching, and strengthening will remedy the problem.

FRIDAY, FEBRUARY 5

Morning workout
▶ Easy 60-minute run

Total miles: 9

Legs felt pretty good. Looking forward to my first marathon simulation tomorrow.

Afternoon workout
▶ Easy 30-minute run

Total miles: 4

Legs felt even better. Ready to run.

SATURDAY, FEBRUARY 6

Morning workout
▶ Marathon simulation

Total miles: 22

Legs felt cold and tight today. Wasn't the workout I was hoping for. Ran

---

* Gluteus medius, a muscle in the buttocks

the first ten miles in 57:30 (5:45 pace), the next eight in 41:27 (5:10 pace), and the last four in 23:40 (5:54 pace).

I underestimated the conditions today. Went out in just half tights and long socks (that were too big and kept falling down). Should have been in full thick tights for the first ten miles and then full thin tights for the tempo. Wore a short-sleeved shirt, arm warmers, and a long-sleeved shirt with thick mitten gloves and a thick knit cap, and I was still cold. The temperature was 22 with a wind chill of 11. I thought I would warm up, but I never did until I put thick tights on during the last four miles. The strong headwind made for brutal conditions. Good learning experience. Now I know how to dress if these conditions come up on race day, even though I doubt it gets this cold in April.

TRAINING IN ALL SEASONS

I prefer summer and fall training in the mountains, but I have learned to put up with the cold winters, knowing that running in various weather conditions presents various challenges that make me stronger. My best races have come in the early spring after enduring a hard winter of running with YakTrax (chains for shoes) on the snowy roads. Still, the Mammoth Lakes winter can be frustrating. We are blessed to be able to drive just 30 minutes south of Mammoth and get out of the cold for workouts.

With a little gear, I can escape the treadmill and run through the winter. A nice windbreaker takes the edge off a cold breeze. The Yaktrax are lightweight and easy to put on and take off. Layers keep me comfortable as my body adjusts to changing temperatures.

Training for the 2008 Olympic Marathon included preparing for extremely hot conditions. I worked for months to train my body to take in more fluids during the run. Hydration is the most important way to deal with running in the heat. Go into the run well hydrated, drink often, and drink plenty after.

My legs felt good, but I just couldn't get them to loosen up to go any faster, and the headwind felt very impeding. Good to know how drastically the conditions can affect the pace. Running 5:10 pace felt hard. I got my butt kicked from mile 15.5 to mile 16.5. It's the longest gradual climb on the course—the toughest section of the course in my opinion. You do get a nice break, however, before heading to the fire station and the hills of Newton. So good to learn the ins and outs of the course.

Big Andy is here. He travels to many of the USA Track and Field meets and is in town for the upcoming indoor meet that Sara competes in tonight. He cranked on my legs and loosened everything up. I felt much better after that. Man, he works hard, but my legs always feel way looser afterward.

Rested in the afternoon and watched Sara race. She ran a good 3000 meters—8:55 and fifth place against a strong field. She was wanting more but looked great and finished well. I'm excited for her and her great start to the year.

It was a little unnerving for me to watch the U.S. men run such a fast 5k (an indoor American record). It's good though. It makes me realize that my heart still needs some work so I can watch other people succeed in my sport and not be threatened by their performances. I want to be able to watch people run fast and be so filled with God and so secure in who I am that I am genuinely happy for them and not envious just because I'm not the one setting records. Galen (13:14) and Bernard (13:11) were rolling tonight!* It looked like fun.

Again, this just shows that I get too much of my self-worth from my performances. I still let the clock tell me how good I am. I still let my splits determine how hopeful I am for the future. I still compare myself to others. But I am getting closer. This is not what running should be all about at its fullest. Running should be a pure flood of joy. Comparing myself to someone else is empty and vain. I rob myself of the goodness and joy of running every time I do it.

---

* Galen Rupp and Bernard Lagat

SUNDAY, FEBRUARY 7

Morning workout
▶ Easy 78-minute run

Total miles: 11

Legs felt surprisingly good. I think it was a combination of the therapy and not being able to push myself as hard as I'd wanted to yesterday because of the conditions. I didn't feel particularly tired after the workout yesterday. Had fun running easy with Sara in Jamaica Plains. Boston has some great areas to run. Coming back here to train would be fun.

In the afternoon, we flew back to San Francisco and will be in Santa Rosa for the next four days before going to Spokane, where Sara will run in the USA Cross-Country Championships. I am excited to see her race again. Looking back on last week makes me realize that yesterday's long run wasn't as far off as I thought. When I get tired, I get very susceptible to thinking negatively and losing hope. I've run slower and slower on my last three tempo runs, but considering they were all done on the road in very different conditions on very different courses, I now see I have no reason to feel as if I'm going backward. Sometimes the course and conditions make times irrelevant.

I have been a little concerned about my fitness with the marathon just ten weeks away. I have struggled a lot with this in the past. I always want to compare my fitness to where I was at in other buildups, and if I am not there, I begin to panic. The truth is, ten weeks is plenty of time. Having room to grow from here is better than hitting my top end of fitness too soon.

Weight is one of my least favorite issues to deal with as a runner. Obviously, a lot of comparison and self-approval issues are involved. I just want to see myself as God sees me and not let my eating habits develop into emotional reactions as they did in college, particularly after poor races or injuries.

Finding the right racing weight is tricky for a marathoner. For the past couple of weeks, I was feeling under-fueled, so I amped it up this week and was feeling much better. However, I think I may have gone to the other extreme and been overly fueled for the long run. My stomach was pretty jacked up, resulting in multiple trips to Dunkin Donuts for bathroom breaks. I want the Holy Spirit to guide my eating habits for the next ten weeks. I want to enjoy food, because I believe Jesus did, yet I want to take the best possible care of myself. Subjecting my eating to a rigid schedule is the easy solution that I've gone to since my college days, but a schedule doesn't allow me to listen to my body and let it tell me when it needs fuel. Rather than eating when I am hungry at 11 a.m., I find myself fighting off the hunger because I am scheduled to eat at noon. I haven't been good at listening to my body.

Week Five

TEN
WEEKS TO BOSTON

MONDAY, FEBRUARY 8

Morning workout
▶ Easy 75-minute run

Total miles: 11

"I hate my job." The words felt all wrong as I finally let the frustration out of my mind and my mouth. I knew I shouldn't say it because I am so blessed to be doing the job I have always dreamed of doing. While others are pounding nails on a roof or sitting behind a desk from nine to five, I am "working" on an easy jog with my wife at 9:30 a.m. in a beautiful park—and saying that I hate my line of work! But sometimes running seems like a difficult career.

It's not just the physical demands. It's the emotional toll that comes when you invest everything and sometimes don't see any progress. Today I was just feeling down, discouraged, and heavy in spirit.

WEEKLY MILEAGE

In high school, I was the mileage king. I loved the sense of accomplishment I felt when I added up my weekly mileage. Sometimes I would even sneak out for an easy extra run so I could hit a nice round number. But now I have learned that running a certain number of miles a week doesn't necessarily mean I will run faster. Running is more art than science. Everyone has unique and changing needs. The only way to know exactly how much is enough but not too much is to experiment and get to know your body as well as you can.

The ideal mileage is the mileage that is right for you. More is not always better. I recommend a gradual progression, trusting that your body will tell you when you have crossed the line and gone too far. While increasing mileage, run on soft surfaces, such as grass and dirt, whenever possible. Also, when increasingly your mileage, alternate longer and shorter weeks.

I am always reluctant to tell people how many miles a week to run. I don't even keep track of my mileage (except when I was writing this journal, and even then I never added up the weekly mileage). I get more confidence from hitting big workouts at specific paces, such as a 15-mile tempo run at five-minute pace at 7000 feet over rolling terrain. My coach's approach has always been to hit the big workouts and then go as short as I need to the following day. I recommend focusing on the workouts and filling in the easy days with as much volume as feels right for your body.

I put on a little weight, but I also felt a heaviness that was hard to shake. I knew I needed to keep my thoughts positive and call on God for help, but nothing seemed to really make a difference. I ran the first 30 minutes feeling frustrated and tempted to call it quits. I seriously thought I might stop and just walk back home. I'd had enough. But then I just kept moving forward. I kept putting one foot in front of the other.

For the last 45 minutes I ran by myself in the mountains, and the healing process finally began. God began to get ahold of me as I zigzagged through the green trees alone in the damp morning sunlight. I started to be more encouraged, and the heaviness began to lift as I connected with God through prayer. Usually God plants a thought in me that gets me out of the funk, but this time I wasn't really hearing anything. God simply lifted the heavy spirit that had been on me since I woke up in the middle of the night. I came home from the run refreshed and ready to begin the ten-week push to Boston. Sometimes I wonder if many of my emotional lows come from running high-volume, high-intensity weeks during my buildups.

Afternoon workout
▶ 45-minute run
▶ Drills and 80-meter strides

Total miles: 6.5

Moved along at a little faster pace. Legs felt much better, and so did my spirit. I'm learning to let the joy come out, even on the difficult days.

TUESDAY, FEBRUARY 9

Morning workout
▶ Warm-up
▶ 2 miles in 9:10 with 4-minute rest
▶ 6 by 800 at 2:14 with 90-second rests, followed by a 4-minute rest
▶ 2 miles in 9:10
▶ Cooldown

Total miles: 13

Man, I needed this one. After the mental struggle I have had the last couple of days, I really needed to get some momentum back. Legs felt really good. Ran around Serra Loop on my old stomping grounds at Stanford. This was about as fast as I have run this two-mile loop. Feeling a lot better about things now. Still frustrated that so much of my momentum is based on my workout performances. Good for me to see that even though I am in good shape, when I run on new or hilly courses—or when it's hot, cold, or windy—I am going to run slower. I need to not get worked up about not running fast every time.

I'm even more convinced now that I need to go to Boston in March to get better acquainted with the course. Running today on Serra Loop really helped because I had worked out on it so many times before and knew exactly what to expect. Just being familiar with the surroundings at Boston will keep me from feeling as if I am running along out in the middle of nowhere. This is exactly what I liked about the 2008 Olympic trials criterion-style course, where we did four loops around Central Park. I always knew where I was at and what to expect. I need to have this same awareness in Boston.

Did five minutes of core exercises (a plank routine). Since I am not doing any other weights, I am going to start doing five minutes of core work after all my morning runs. It's going to be important to have a strong core and back to handle the ups and downs of the Boston course.

Afternoon workout
▶ 40-minute run
Total miles: 6

Not the most scenic run. I ran in an industrial area of Santa Rosa while I was getting a truck bed cover installed on my Nissan Titan, but I still felt pretty good.

WEDNESDAY, FEBRUARY 10

Morning workout
▶ Easy 75-minute run
Total miles: 11

Legs felt pretty good. I was a little sore from a massage yesterday, but my legs felt like they responded well to yesterday's workout. It's crazy how I can feel when my legs are absorbing the workouts. Improvement is around the corner!

Afternoon workout
▶ Easy 45-minute run
Total miles: 6.5

Legs felt good. Stomach is still jacked up. I think it might be from the multivitamins I am taking with lunch. I'm going to try not taking supplements till after my second run and see how that goes.

Read Romans 12 this morning. Love this:

> Therefore, I urge you, brothers, in view of God's mercy, to offer your bodies as living sacrifices, holy and pleasing to God—this is your spiritual act of worship. Do not conform any longer to the pattern of this world, but be transformed by the renewing of your mind. Then you will be able to test and approve what God's will is—his good, pleasing and perfect will.*

That's exactly what I want to do in my day-to-day training: offer my body up to God so He can use it as He wills. This also captures the change in perspective I am so desperate for. I need this renewal of mind so running isn't all about winning, performances, and times, yet I still feel as if I have a long way to go. I saw a post–Super Bowl commercial recently that showed Drew Brees immediately after the game saying that he was going to Disney World. I thought to myself that only one person got to be Drew Brees this year, to reach the pinnacle of his sport at his position, and that everyone else "failed" because there can be only one winner.

REST

Rest is probably the most underemphasized aspect of training. Your body's physical adaptation takes place when resting.

Many people are simply not confident enough to rest—I know I wasn't. Even now, when I am feeling insecure about my fitness, I press harder in workouts and on easy runs. As a result, I don't recover enough, and I get more and more run-down and tired.

I often sleep eight to ten hours a night and then take a one- or two-hour nap. When I make sleep a priority, my body is able to handle a much greater workload than it otherwise could. In addition, I try to stay off my legs as much as possible during the day when I am not running, especially on the last few days leading up to a race.

---

* Verses 1-3 NIV

I really struggle with the concept of having only one winner. I don't want to tell kids that if they do their best, dream big, work hard, and sacrifice, they will accomplish their dreams. If their dream is to win the Super Bowl, they will probably never accomplish it. Instead, I want to encourage kids to focus, work hard, and dream big because the journey is what matters. To dream and live a life of devotion is better than to never dream at all. As we pursue our dreams, we realize the abundant life.

THURSDAY, FEBRUARY 11

Morning workout
- ▶ 20-minute warm-up
- ▶ 40-minute fartlek run
- ▶ 20-minute cooldown

Total miles: 13

I love getting up early and pounding away on the beautiful, hilly trails of Santa Rosa. I have no idea about the pace or the exact distance, but I was moving along pretty good the whole time.

While I was out running, I felt that familiar feeling that I was made to win the Boston Marathon. I remind myself that it can't be all about winning and losing, but I want to accomplish the purpose for which God created me, and I believe part of my unique purpose is to win the Boston Marathon. I don't know when it will happen, but I believe it will happen.

I see myself winning the race. I see myself racing with joy over the hills of Newton, soaring with God as I have from time to time during my career. I can't wait to taste it.

I'm reading a really good book right now—*Born to Run*. It describes a tribe of "supernatural" runners hidden out in the bush in Mexico. I'm currently reading the part about coach Joe Vigil, whom I know and who coached my coach, as he watches this tribe race an ultramarathon. He comes to the conclusion that these runners succeed simply because of their joy of running. They love to run. This is exactly what I have been desiring so strongly in my training.

It's all about loving the simple act of running. In America, getting caught up in times, places, and so on is all too easy, but the goal really is just to love the simple act of running. Of course, competition has its place in events like the Boston Marathon and others, but while I am out there on the road, it all has to come back to simply letting the joy of running flow. The joy of knowing I am doing what God made me to do. The joy of going after the purpose for which I was created. Jesus endured because of His joy: "Let us run with endurance the race that is set before us, fixing our eyes on Jesus, the author and perfecter of faith, who for the joy set before Him endured the cross."* And so did the Israelites: "The joy of the LORD is your strength."† Joy is the ultimate requirement for triumphing in the difficult journey ahead.

Afternoon workout
▶ 40-minute run
Total miles: 6

Legs felt a little like Jell-O from the flight to Spokane. Ran on the cross-country course with Sara. One of the upsides of our job is traveling the world together and checking out new and beautiful places like Spokane.

FRIDAY, FEBRUARY 12

Morning workout
▶ 45-minute run
Total miles: 7

Legs are continuing to come around. Felt good. Starting to move along a little more on my easy runs without trying harder. This is always a good sign for me that my training is taking hold. Feeling more pop off the ground.

---

* Hebrews 12:1-2
† Nehemiah 8:10

Afternoon workout
▶ 75-minute run

Total miles: 11.5

Glad I am not running cross-country this weekend. Running on grass is not my forte. I feel as if I'm melting into the grass with every step. After half an hour of running on the grass, it was a breath of fresh air to get on Centennial Path, which runs near the course. Legs felt remarkably good. Starting to get more and more excited about how things are going. I don't have the usual nags and pains that I have become accustomed to when walking down stairs or bending over to pick up something.

Watched the opening ceremonies for the winter Olympics without any emotional pain—a good sign that I have moved on from my Olympic disappointment in 2008. I am excited for London 2012. I will be a much more mature and secure runner by then. I have certainly learned a lot about the marathon.

SATURDAY, FEBRUARY 13

Morning workout
▶ 70-minute run

Total miles: 11

Ran along the river path with Coach. Felt even better than yesterday. My legs feel fluid, open, and breathing. I have been thinking a lot about enjoying the feeling of running rather than focusing on completing the run. Nice to feel good and to get some momentum going.

Excited to watch Sara compete in the cross-country championships today. She is fit and ready to go. It is great to see her running so strong after struggling last season.

I think my increased running volume is doing good things for my legs. I was half expecting, or even scared, that the extra volume would further deaden my legs, but it has done just the opposite. My legs have more life in them than they have in a long, long time. Maybe they needed to break out of the usual routine and mileage to compensate for the heightened workload. Not sure if this is a good explanation or if I am just starting to come around naturally. Running is a mystery at times.

Afternoon workout
▶ 45-minute run

Total miles: 7

Legs feel good despite an active day of running around the cross-country course.

Watching Sara run is inspiring. I am always impressed watching her when the race isn't coming easily but she still runs tough and does the best she can with what she has. Runners who press through like that inspire me more than winners who float along effortlessly to victory. Anyone can run on good days. But when things aren't really clicking and we still get everything out of our body that we can muster, our character shows.

SUNDAY, FEBRUARY 14

Morning workout
▶ Marathon simulation: 10 miles medium hard, 8-mile tempo run
▶ Cooldown

Total miles: 22

On the muddy single tracks in Annadel State Park (Santa Rosa), I ran ten miles in 59:30 (5:57 pace), an eight-mile tempo run in 38:24 (4:48 pace), and a *slow* four-mile cooldown. Felt like a million bucks! Enjoying the simple act of running was easy today. Had a pop in my legs that I haven't felt in my tempo runs for a while. Hard to believe I was struggling to run sub-5:10 miles a week ago in Boston. If I continue to improve like this, who knows what's possible!

Feeling more and more as if something special is around the corner. Driving back home to Mammoth in the afternoon. Hoping not to find an insane amount of snow, frozen pipes, and water running throughout our house.

Week Six

NINE
WEEKS TO BOSTON

MONDAY, FEBRUARY 15

Morning workout
▶ Easy 60-minute run
Total miles: 8

Back in Mammoth training with the team after an extended break. Legs still felt like they have some juice in them, which means I didn't go too hard yesterday. Ran with Sara nice and easy. The altitude didn't feel too hard.

Afternoon workout
▶ 50-minute run
Total miles: 7

Legs felt really good. Moved along a bit. Had fun running with Sara and Josh. Continuing to enjoy the higher volume.

TUESDAY, FEBRUARY 16

Morning workout
▶ Warm-up
▶ Intervals: 10 by 1k at 2:55
▶ Cooldown
Total miles: 12.2

Ran a fast 400 (65 seconds) in the middle of every other interval. Legs started out feeling good and got even better as I went. Even floated along a bit in the cooldown because my legs didn't feel like jogging.

Afternoon workout
▶ 48-minute run
Total miles: 7

Moved along again. Legs still feeling good. I'm loving how I'm progressing right now. Still not sure exactly what is making me feel so much better all a sudden, but I'm thankful for it. I have been doing self-ART* on the foam roller and have been more conscientious about doing active stretching. I've also even been experimenting with eating less meat and more plant-based protein.

TAPERING TRAINING INTO RACES

I am always amazed by the difference between what I am able to do in practice and what I am able to do in a race. I may be able to run only two-thirds of the race distance at race pace in practice. What is it about race day that allows me to find that extra third? Race-day excitement helps, but the taper is what makes up for a majority of this distance.

A good rule of thumb is to cut down your total overall volume by at least 25 percent. Andy Gerard, one of my coaches from Stanford, used to tell me that my body was used to a certain amount of volume and intensity of workouts, so rather than completely eliminating workouts, I just needed to scale them back. When I was getting ready for the NCAA Track and Field Championships, instead of running 10 by 1000 meters in a workout, I would run 8 by 1000 meters. This helped keep my legs from going stale before the race, which can often happen with too much rest.

When designing a taper, as with so many other things in running, you may be tempted to think more is better. Training for a marathon, my volume gets very high, so I might reduce my volume as much as 50 percent or more on race week. However, for those running less than 75 miles

---

* Active release technique

a week, I recommend experimenting with a 25 percent reduction. Like most aspects of running, the taper is highly individualized and will require some experimentation and tinkering.

Many people completely cut their speed and tempo workouts during their taper, which is exactly the opposite of what they should do. Taper week is a great time to do extra drills and easy strides to get the legs firing. On race week, make sure to continue the workouts you are accustomed to. Just make them shorter.

Tapering presents a huge mental challenge. When I am months away from the year's biggest race, I picture myself floating through runs and workouts on the last week before the event. These fantasies rarely materialize. To fight the temptation to question my fitness, I remember that the way I feel on a particular workout is not as important as all the training I've done in the months before race week.

WEDNESDAY, FEBRUARY 17

Morning workout
▶ Long, easy run (1 hour, 46 minutes)
Total miles: 16

Legs felt really good for the first 50 minutes and then kind of back to the way I have been feeling. It was hard to enjoy running with the guys on the team once I started feeling bad. I don't like the sensation of trying to hang on during easy runs. When I am feeling sluggish, I'd rather take it easy on my own. Watching everyone else run away from me is trying on my confidence. I just keep reminding myself of the many tired days I had before I ran my best marathons.

THURSDAY, FEBRUARY 18

Morning workout
▶ Easy 75-minute run
Total miles: 10

Legs felt pretty good.

Afternoon workout
▶ Easy 45-minute run
Total miles: 6.5

Glad to have another afternoon run logged.

FRIDAY, FEBRUARY 19

Morning workout
▶ 20-minute warm-up
▶ 12-mile tempo run
▶ 20-minute cooldown
Total miles: 18

A solid run today. Nothing too fast, but it was good enough to set me up well for the weeks to come. Averaged around five minutes per mile.

Afternoon workout
▶ Easy 40-minute run
Total miles: 5.5

Legs felt a little tired from this morning.

SATURDAY, FEBRUARY 20

Morning workout
▶ Easy 75-minute run

Total miles: 11

Legs felt surprisingly good. Having some pop in my legs is always nice the day after a hard workout. It means that I ran the right effort level and still have more to go after in the weeks to come. Not bad running down by the airport. Was able to stay mostly soft on the shoulder of the road. Nice day here in Mammoth.

Afternoon workout
▶ Easy 45-minute run

Total miles: 6.5 miles

Legs felt solid again. Stomach was a little jacked up from putting down a brown rice bread sandwich moments before the run. It is amazing how the stomach affects the way my legs feel and move. Still need to learn more about what afternoon snacks I can get away with before runs. Brown rice bread is tasty but needs a little more digestion time.

RECOVERING AFTER RACES

After winning the 2008 Olympic Marathon trials in New York, I was so excited, I didn't cool down, get a massage, or get in the ice bath. The following day I didn't jog. Instead, Sara and I hopped on a plane for a rewarding vacation to Israel. I took my two-week customary break: no running, no cross training, no exercise. I just enjoyed being a normal person for a couple of weeks—a perfectly healthy thing for me to do.

I will never forget my first run back. I was practically crippled. I have never felt so debilitated in my entire life. Slowly jogging three miles was harder than the race two weeks prior. My legs were stiff, tight, and extremely inflexible. My wife couldn't help but laugh as I struggled to jog 10-minute miles. A passerby would never have thought I had qualified for the Olympics just two weeks earlier. Only after two weeks of jogging, massage, stretching, and doing strides was I finally able to run at a normal pace. I learned that I haven't finished a race until I recover properly.

Now I kick-start my recovery by immediately drinking a recovery shake, yielding approximately 350 calories of complex carbohydrates and high-quality protein. A recovery meal 30 to 60 minutes after exercise is essential if the body is to recover effectively. I also get a massage immediately after the race or use a foam roller and softball to do some self-massage if no massage therapist is available. After the massage I do some stretching and take an ice bath in my hotel room.

Rather than starting my two-week break the day after the race, I go out for a run the morning after the race. The 30-minute shakeout run starts slowly and painfully, but usually by the end of it I'm feeling good and my legs have processed much of the junk and tightness that I put into them the previous day. Now I am ready for my two weeks of rest.

SUNDAY, FEBRUARY 21

Morning workout
▶ Long run (2 hours, 15 minutes—5:43 pace)

Total miles: 23.75

Legs felt really good today. Felt like I had the nutrition and hydration working pretty well despite having to stop for a bathroom break at 90 minutes. Took down a lot of data including blood glucose and lactate before, during, and after the long run.

Had a lot of fun out there, which was easy because my legs were feeling so great. After taking the first couple of miles to ease into the run, I was surprised to look down and see mid 5:30 splits mile after mile. That pace hasn't felt this easy in a while. Legs did fatigue after about two hours, but that is to be expected. Ninety minutes into the run, I ran ten by two minutes at half-marathon pace and climbed some good hills. The limiting factor seemed to be the flexibility in my hamstrings. Felt like they were getting all gummed up and restricted after 1:45 of running. Good practice to work through this and even better to realize I still need to hit the self-therapy and ART hard to get my legs as clean as possible over the next eight weeks. Still, I'm very excited about how I'm feeling and where my current fitness is at.

Sang "Hallelujah Song" in church tonight and had visions of Boston. I saw myself laughing as I ran down Boylston effortlessly, swerving like a plane from side to side and celebrating God's goodness. Joy flowed out of me because I tasted God's goodness. My legs pedaled effortlessly as fast as I wanted them to go. No resistance, no hard breathing, just peaceful, effortless, heavenly running. It was so sweet. I saw myself singing the Hallelujah Chorus as I finished, picking up Sara, running joyously on the streets, and celebrating the goodness of God. I felt that God was telling me to run as if I couldn't mess up the race, as if I could do no wrong. Completely free, like a bird floating on the thermal currents of air.

Speaking of the word *hallelujah*, two years ago our Asics rep came up with the idea of putting it on a shirt. Asics will be offering it in their catalog. Now, *there's* a prophetic word from someone who probably didn't even realize he was giving it. Prophecy speaks of our potential when we partner with God, and I hope to fulfill this prophetic word by running joyfully. After all, *hallelujah* is a biblical expression of joy. I believe I will sing the Hallelujah Chorus on Boylston.

Week Seven

EIGHT
WEEKS TO BOSTON

STEPS
FOUNDATION

asics

USA

MONDAY, FEBRUARY 22

Morning workout
▶ Very easy 70-minute run

Total miles: 9

Legs felt a little tired today, and I had some trouble moving along through the eight inches of fresh snow. Felt a little better as the run progressed. Still enjoyed running with Sara. The winter in Mammoth is not always fun, but it's strikingly beautiful.

Had the craziest dream last night. It is not unusual for me to dream about races. I'm usually getting beat by a girl, forgetting my racing shoes, or running in slow motion. But I have other dreams that feel so real that I pay close attention to them. They are such emotional experiences that when I wake up, my heart is racing.

Last night I had one of these dreams. I dreamed that I won the Boston Marathon. I don't remember all the ins and outs of the dream, but I remember being honored for winning and being so overcome by emotion that I couldn't say anything. I was completely humbled because God had chosen to satisfy my heart's desire and because I had tasted so deeply of His goodness. I had done what God created me to do at this point in my life, and I felt so deeply satisfied and full that all I could do was weep. I feel that way at speaking engagements when the host group plays a clip from the Olympic trials, but in my dream, the feeling was even more intense. I sensed God's pleasure as He watched with pride as I do what I do—for Him.

Afternoon workout
▶ 30-minute warm-up
▶ Hill sprints: 10 by 30 meters
Total miles: 4

This afternoon I was in a bit of a funk. I don't know why I was in a bad mood. I napped for two hours and fifteen minutes and woke up refreshed but also a little out of it. I always feel the most tired on Mondays, which is to be expected after hammering out a long run the day before. A case of the Mondays, as they say. I'm walking the fine line between training and overtraining. The good news is that Tuesday always comes, and I always feel much better then.

TUESDAY, FEBRUARY 23

Morning workout
▶ 20-minute warm-up with drills and strides
▶ 2 miles, 4-minutes rest, 1 mile, repeat
▶ 20-minute cooldown
Total miles: 12

In the first fast set, I ran the two miles in 9:19 and the one mile (slightly uphill) in 4:35. In the second set, I ran the two miles in 9:14 and the one mile (slightly downhill) in 4:28. Ran the first set by myself and felt solid. The mile coming back up was hard. I felt pretty drained after that, but Alistair joined me for the second set, and I felt much better. Running with someone is sometimes amazingly easier than running alone. I think the key to running with someone is to be relaxed and to be secure enough to allow him to run faster than me if he needs to, to not feel as if I need to respond to every little gap that may open up. A tricky mind-set indeed.

Felt better and better as the workout progressed. Finished well (last 400 of the mile in 64 seconds). Good to know I can still turn it over even when I am slightly tired coming into the workout. It's going to be a good week. Glad Monday is behind me.

Afternoon workout

▶ Easy 40-minute run

Total miles: 6

Legs and body felt a little tired. Glad to be getting a massage from Andrew. Continuing to think about having joy in every moment whether I am feeling like a million bucks or struggling. Living out of a joyful heart brings so much power and fullness to my life and running.

For dinner we went to Deena's house for some typically ridiculous food. Fun to share such a wonderful meal with good people. Carrie, Josh's wife, practiced a hairstyle and makeup on me for an upcoming photo shoot. Can't say I like wearing makeup, but it is good to have someone who won't make me look plastic, as often happens when I get hair and makeup done for photo shoots.

STRETCHING

Stretching has long been a hot topic among distance runners. I don't do any static stretching. I have found that the best way for me to stay relatively loose and injury free is to incorporate dynamic and active stretching into my daily routine. Every morning before I run, I do a dynamic flexibility routine that includes leg swings, hurdle exchanges, and other similar exercises to get my legs loosened up after a night's sleep. After the run, I spend 30 to 45 minutes doing self-massage with a roller and softball and then do more active stretching.

Active stretching activates the muscle opposite the one you are trying to stretch. For example, lie on your back while holding a rope that is looped around your right foot. Use your right quad to bring your right leg straight up with the knee strong but not quite locked. When you get as far as your leg will naturally go in the air, use the rope to pull your leg a few inches farther. You should feel a deep but not trembling stretch in your right hamstring. Try to keep the rest of your body lying flat on the ground.

How much should I change my appearance for photo shoots? I realize that my sponsors pay my bills and help me do what I love to do for a job (for which I am incredibly grateful), so I usually shave the beard and trim the hair for photo shoots and races so I look more respectable. But sometimes in training I need to use little mental edges to enhance my performance. For example, I like to grow out my hair and beard and then cut it the night before a race (a tradition that dates back to my high-school days). I realize that the physiological benefit is nil, but the psychological effect is real. Right now I'm in the mountains and training like Rocky, so I'm really feeling the beard and long hair. I may even keep the long hair for Boston, but certainly not the beard—although maybe, come to think of it, I'll keep a Lasse Viren beard.* I realize some people won't understand, but the last eight weeks before Boston are mine. I get to be totally me, all the time.

WEDNESDAY, FEBRUARY 24

Morning workout
▶ Easy 82-minute run
Total miles: 12

"Why do we live here? We could train anywhere in the world—Mexico, Columbia, Kenya—and yet we train here! Why?" I yelled as I slipped for the fifth time in that many minutes running through a blizzard with the team on Mammoth Scenic Loop (a quiet paved road just a mile from our home). I knew I had a bad attitude, but I couldn't hold it in anymore. It was dumping snow, and with every slip I saw my journey to Boston crashing to a halt because of muscle spasms. I was sure I'd tear something before long.

Even our tried-and-true Yaktrax were failing me because the wet snow was gumming them up. I had skates for shoes, running on top of six inches of fresh snow, on top of ice. It was like trying to run on one of those Power Glide exercisers where you put special socks over your shoes and slide back and forth like a speed skater. I'm glad Josh was running next to me.

---

* Lasse Viren won four Olympic gold medals running for Finland while sporting an awesome beard.

He understood my frustration, and I felt comfortable venting around him. Eventually, he gently pulled me out of it. I think the best way to help bring someone out of a bad mood is to let them vent but then infect their attitude with your positive attitude. By the end of the run I was in better spirits.

Part of my bad attitude had to do with my right hamstring feeling really tight on the outside. I hope it doesn't develop into something I shouldn't run through. Before NYC last year, a little hamstring tightness turned into an eight-week battle. I was getting 90 minutes of massage every day from Leah, a massage therapist we brought up to Mammoth for the ten weeks leading up to NYC. Still, during every run, I was thinking about the pain coming from my hamstring. I couldn't run a single stride at marathon pace the day before my tune-up half-marathon in Philadelphia. It was a miracle I made it through that race. I even tried acupuncture for the first time—two days prior to the race in a sketchy area of Chinatown in Philly. I don't know if it helped or not, but by the grace of God, I won the race, running my last mile in 4:26. Finally, a couple weeks before the NYC, I stopped feeling it.

Leah was a great addition to the team. She is a healer in my opinion. I believe God has given her the gift of touch to bring healing to the body. She is just a normal lady living in Big Bear, but she really is an amazing massage therapist. She used to travel with Lennox Lewis* and work on him before his big fights. Leah worked on me before my buildup to London '08.

I found that Leah's work was very helpful, and getting worked on so frequently was very relaxing. But I learned that certain types of therapies are more effective than others with certain kinds of injuries. Despite all the therapy, I battled the hamstring issue for eight weeks. And in the race itself, I came down with a nasty tightness in my right glut med that made NYC my physically toughest marathon. Leah's work helped me train and race at a higher level, but I wasn't bulletproof. I am thankful for the love Leah poured into my body for those ten weeks.

---

* Three-time world heavyweight boxing champion

I walked away from the whole NYC experience believing that God has His ways, and though I don't always understand why He works the way He does, He is always good and His intent for us is always good. I don't believe God brought those injuries on me. I believe He wanted to heal me from them but didn't for some reason.

God is still good, and I still trust in Him just as Meb has unswervingly trusted in God's plan through the good and bad since picking up a medal in the 2004 Olympic Marathon and then struggling for years, even failing to make the 2008 team. I believe my day will come. I just need to patiently and expectantly wait for it. "Though it tarries, wait for it; for it will certainly come, it will not delay."* "Those who wait on the LORD shall renew their strength; they shall mount up with wings like eagles, they shall run and not be weary, they shall walk and not faint."† I'm holding on to what I believe God has promised to me. I'm a laid-back California type who likes to let things happen, but I have a proactive role in realizing my God-given potential—to actively believe God's promises day by day.

THURSDAY, FEBRUARY 25

Morning workout
▶ 20-minute warm-up
▶ Intervals: 3 by 20-minutes (uphill)
    with 2-minute downhill recoveries
▶ 10-minute cooldown

Total miles: 14.5

Legs felt good today. Ran with my Garmin and my heart-rate monitor. Kept my heart rate between 165 and 175 during the intervals. Mostly stayed around 168 till the last ten minutes or so. Good to get the data. Averaged 6:24 pace (including the recovery jogging). I think this is pretty solid, but I can't remember any data from similar workouts. I dropped

---

* Habakkuk 2:3

† Isaiah 40:31

nearly three pounds in water weight in an hour and fourteen minutes of running (including the cooldown) in 42-degree temperatures.

Still learning to let the joy flow out of me even if I'm not hitting home runs yet. A month from now, I will run this uphill run much faster, but I'm happy with where I'm at right now. My training is continuing to click.

Afternoon workout
▶ Easy 30-minute run
▶ Strides: 6 by 100 meters
Total miles: 4.5

Traveled to Albuquerque for Sara's race at the U.S. Indoor Track and Field Championships. Felt a lot better after the strides. Legs loosened up nicely after the long travel from Mammoth. Definitely felt like Jell-O at first.

FRIDAY, FEBRUARY 26

Morning workout
▶ Easy 75-minute run
Total miles: 11

Legs felt really good despite the travel. Woke up this morning with a tickling sensation in my throat. Hoping my body can fight this one off as I have been killing the water and getting in some vitamin C. Colds are the worst. Mine usually hang on for two weeks, especially when I start coughing up phlegm. Trying to stay mentally positive and use that positive energy to fight it off.

Afternoon workout
▶ Easy 45-minute run
Total miles: 6

Legs felt great. Figuring out that I'm not drinking enough water to aid in digestion, which has caused me to suffer stomach problems on many of my afternoon runs. Excited for tomorrow's workout. Still feeling a little cough and starting to hack up some stuff. Not much I can do at this point.

SATURDAY, FEBRUARY 27

Morning workout
▶ Marathon simulation: 10 miles at 5:45 pace
▶ 10 miles at 5:14 pace
▶ 2-mile cooldown

Total miles: 22

Windy day here in Albuquerque at 6000 feet. I felt strong today, and I know I have a lot more inside of me. It's a good sign that I can still have a solid day out there even when the conditions aren't quite right, I'm in a new place, I'm fighting off a little cold, and I'm in the middle of a high-volume week with only one day to recover between hard workouts. Solid week this week.

I feel increasingly thankful for whatever performances come my way in practice. Today's run included some painful miles (5:22, 5:35) running into the wind when I felt like stopping or just checking out mentally, but I saw myself in Boston running into the wind and doing well. I was able to rally for a good couple of miles at the end. My body definitely feels a little off, as I would expect when it's fighting a cold. Being 1 or 2 percent on or off makes all the difference. I know there is so much more in me. Looking forward to kicking this cold and letting my fitness out over the next seven weeks before Boston. Can't believe how close we are getting.

CROSS TRAINING

The best cross training for a runner is running. I always encourage people to run as much as their body allows, as I believe this is the best way to improve. However, many people (myself included!) are sometimes plagued with injuries or other factors that prohibit running. There are many cross-training alternatives, so go with something you enjoy.

Sara was battling an injury during an indoor season at Stanford and had to take some time off from running. She chose to sign up for some spinning classes. After a few weeks of spinning, she had maintained her fitness and perhaps even added to it. She ended up having a great indoor season just a few weeks after getting off the bike and getting back on the track.

You can mimic the same effect in a pool. Before the 2008 Olympics I spent a few days on the underwater treadmill at the Mammoth Hospital SPORT Center, which is the best system for running underwater but may be hard to find. I have done some aqua jogging—running in a pool. Other effective cross-training options include elliptical workouts and biking.

The key with cross training is getting out there and actually doing it. I struggle with motivation when injuries occur. Getting on a machine is often the last thing I feel like doing. However, just a half hour to an hour a day can go a long way in maintaining fitness. When your body is ready to run again, you will certainly be glad you overcame a lack of motivation and did your cross training.

Cross training may also be the way for you to avoid injury when increasing mileage. Consider biking instead of doing some of your easy runs to give your legs a break from the pounding.

Later this afternoon I watched Sara run an exciting 3000 at the Indoor National Championships. She finished second by inches. Looks like she is off to Doha, Qatar, for the World Indoor Championships next week.

SUNDAY, FEBRUARY 28

Took the day off. Woke up and immediately went to the bathroom to cough up the green phlegm that I was dreading. My cold symptoms definitely turned a corner into a full-blown virus. I have had this one before.

It is usually a two-week battle before I feel completely better. I started feeling it on Wednesday, so I probably have about ten more days unless God intervenes. Praying and believing God for just that. I just pray that my body would be as it is in heaven. I know God can heal me.

It is a bummer having to take a day off. I was not happy when Coach gave me the orders, but I know it is probably best. I usually don't take any days off, so perhaps the day off will kick the cold quicker than my typical two-week bout. I knew I was off yesterday. My legs have been feeling so good this week, but my body is not cooperating and letting me get out the fitness I know is in there.

It's frustrating because I have only seven weeks now. It's time to start hitting some good workouts. I have had a couple of decent workouts, but I really haven't nailed one yet. I recently decided with Coach and Sara to spend only three weeks in Boston before the race, so I only have four weeks left in Mammoth to really hone my fitness, and then I'll have a week to hit it hard in Boston before it's time to start resting. I'm hungry for breakthrough! I think this will be a good heart check for me to make sure I still have "open hands" in regard to Boston. It is so easy to start wanting it too much.

I know that my only obsession should be following Christ, but when my whole day, week, month, and year is built around hitting two big marathons, it becomes the ultimate challenge to not make life all about those two days. Things like sickness, injury, and disappointment provide opportunities for me to look into my heart and make sure I am in the right place. Is my treasure in heaven, or has my treasure become these two races a year? A heart check like this isn't fun, but it's necessary if I am to live the good life that flows from a heart that's in the right place.

Week Eight

SEVEN
WEEKS TO BOSTON

MONDAY, MARCH 1

Morning workout
▶ Easy 75-minute run with strides
Total miles: 11

My body felt pretty good, but my lungs feel restricted and full of fluid. Nevertheless, felt great to run again.

Afternoon workout
▶ Easy 45-minute run
Total miles: 6

Rough travel day today. Three flights to get back to Mammoth. Traveling when I'm sick isn't fun. My body was feeling out of it, but I felt much better running when we got home. I can't tell if it's better to run through colds or take days off. I often feel better after I run and get the junk out of my lungs. Took it easy.

TUESDAY, MARCH 2

Morning workout
▶ 20-minute warm-up with drills and strides
▶ Intervals: 10 by 1000 meters with a 66-second 400
    in the middle of every other one
▶ 20-minute cooldown

Total miles: 12

Had to take the edge off the workout. My legs felt good, but I had a hard time breathing. Lungs and chest feel terrible. I hacked up stuff before, during, and after the workout. It's hard to have fun when I feel sick, but I'm happy to make it through the workout.

Afternoon workout
▶ Easy 45-minute run

Total miles: 7

Legs felt good, so I moved a long a bit, but my breathing and lungs are still a mess. Busy day today. Didn't get back from the morning workout until just before a conference call with Nissan at one p.m. Had an interview with a Christian church for a video at two, ran at three, massage at four, and then hit the steam room to try to sweat this cold out.

I have no idea what I was doing in the steam room. Without checking to see how hot the room already was, I just flicked the switch on for ten minutes and headed in. When I went in another guy was already in there and stomped out, apparently miffed that someone had turned the steamer on. Another hippy guy came in and sat next to me as it got really, really hot and steamy. I looked over a couple minutes later and the guy had left. I had to step out before the ten minutes were up, and he was in the hot tub and said, "Dude, that steam room was intense. I felt like my skin was burning off." I just laughed to myself and headed back in.

I really like the steam room to sweat out the toxins and clear all the junk out of the system, although I had to pound the water to rehydrate. Felt much better after.

INJURIES

When I began training for my first marathon, my massage therapist, Andrew Kastor (Deena Kastor's husband), told me that half the battle of the marathon was getting to the line healthy. He was certainly right. The gold and silver medalists from the previous Olympics had to drop out of my first marathon due to injuries.

The key to injuries is twofold: First, take care of your body to prevent injuries from occurring. Second, when injuries do occur, focus on treating the cause, not just the symptoms. An injury in one area is often caused by a hidden tightness in a completely different area. For example, I have had tight quads pull on my patella. Massage on my quads does help, as does icing my knee (relieving the symptoms), but the real cause was my tight hamstrings, which caused my quads to work too hard. Treating the symptoms is important, but finding and treating the cause will bring healing.

Some injuries (such as stress fractures) are more traumatic and may not be caused by recurring tightness. Use your own judgment and your doctors' input to decide how much rest your body needs. If pain increases the more I run, I don't attempt to run through it.

Of course, the best way to deal with injury is to avoid it. How? I wear only fresh running shoes, get massage or do some self-massage every day, ice my legs in a cold creek after every hard workout, do my best to sleep on my back (I haven't mastered this one yet, but sleeping on my side leaves my hips cranky), use a compression devise called a NormaTec MVP a few times a week, take warm Epsom salt baths, and try to fuel myself with the cleanest fuel possible. Our team also does form drills at least three times a week to reinforce proper form.

We prayed tonight for Sara's trip to Doha tomorrow. It was cool—I could feel God's presence moving in a strong way. I think the Lord has something special for her on this trip. Not sure if it has to do with her performance or a connection with people, but I think it will be a special trip for her.

As we were driving home from dinner, I encouraged Sara to go into the

World Championships with a steadfast heart and an open vision. That is also the heart that I want to have going into Boston. I want to set my heart on praising God and to have an open vision, allowing God to work however He desires. I hold Boston with open hands.

WEDNESDAY, MARCH 3

Morning workout
▶ Easy run (1 hour, 45 minutes)
Total miles: 15

My lungs felt terrible today. Feel as if I'm operating at 50 percent. I still feel strongly that something special inside me is waiting to come out, but I guess it will have to wait a little longer. After the run I felt totally out of it. I can't remember the last time I felt this bad. It was a rough, rough day. I took a two-hour nap when I got home and woke up still feeling really bad. My head was pounding and felt all swollen, my legs were super achy, and I couldn't stop a wheezing cough that killed my lungs every time I hacked. This was really an unproductive day. I was useless while Sara packed. I spent most of the afternoon unable to move, just staring off into space. Unfortunately, this didn't make for too fun of a last day with Sara before she leaves for Doha for nearly two weeks.

I got on some antibiotics today, which I have mixed feelings about. Before the Olympic trials, I got this same nasty cold in Europe and got on antibiotics. When I got home and started my preparation, I really struggled. I'm not sure whether the antibiotics made me feel so bad, but I'm nervous to take them. All I know is I can't go on feeling like this. I didn't even have the energy to go to the steam room or the store.

THURSDAY, MARCH 4

Morning workout
▶ Easy 75-minute run

Total miles: 11

Felt like Lazarus today—back from the dead! After the worst day of sickness ever yesterday, I wasn't sure if the run would happen today. But I woke up refreshed, and though I haven't recovered completely, I at least had the energy to run.

Afternoon workout
▶ Easy 45-minute run

Total miles: 6

Found the perfect 45-minute loop around town today.

Finished this e-mail interview today for *Running Times*. These interview questions are the best I have ever been asked. I really enjoyed writing the responses and poured myself into them. The theme is the theology of God in athletics, which I, naturally, have been very interested in as a Christian athlete.

> *Running Times:* Why do you think God takes an active interest in the outcome of sporting events? Given that the outwardly faithful more often than not don't win, what does that mean about God's involvement in these events?
>
> *Ryan Hall:* "As the heavens are higher than the earth, so are My ways higher than your ways, and My thoughts than your thoughts" (Isaiah 55:9).
>
> I remember very vividly during my senior year in high school after my last chance to break 4:00 in the mile ended in disappointment. I watched my other Christian buddies similarly struggle on the track that afternoon asking why it was that Christian runners seemed to be struggling more than everyone else. It bothered me that here we were, being open about our faith in God, and didn't seem to be getting any

help from God. I would read stories in the Bible about God being so involved in the daily lives of biblical characters. I didn't understand why God didn't seem to be involved in my running. This was the beginning of years of trying to grapple with God's role, not only in my personal running, but also in sports as a whole.

I have heard stories and had personal experiences in my own running when I felt very strongly that God was involved. For example, running the Houston half-marathon and breaking an hour was the easiest race I ever ran. I felt like I could have run another half-marathon despite being in the middle of heavy marathon training, not backing off for the race at all and having the craziest, most stressful travel I have ever had before. But it wasn't just the ease in which I ran that made me feel like God was with me, it was the peace that I felt as I ran.

Even as I struggle to describe the sensation of running with God, I am sure many can relate to the sensation. I have heard similar stories from other athletes of indescribable strength as they competed. I don't doubt their testimonies. However, it didn't ease my frustration to taste God moving through me as I ran and to hear similar stories but not know when God was going to show up. It also intrigued me to watch other Christian athletes saying they were going to knock out so-and-so in the whatever round because God told them this was going to happen only to have the outcome turn out the complete opposite of what God said. I don't doubt that these athletes have the right heart and are trying to hear God leading into their competitions; however, something obviously was getting lost in translation.

From my experience through my running career of weathering many lows and enjoying some really high mountain peak experiences, I have felt that the sweetest part of running is feeling God with me as I run, and the great thing about that is it isn't something that only one person or a couple of people can experience in a race. We can all experience it. We can all feel something that is even sweeter, available every time we toe the line and more lasting than winning or setting a record. Today, whenever I sign my name to an autograph I always write John 10:10 with it because it is the best part of following Jesus and having his Spirit in me—it makes life sweeter. My running is better, my daily life is better, etc. Following Jesus doesn't mean abandoning the fun things of this world; it means having more fun, being free from the worries of daily life, and experiencing things in greater, more fulfilling ways.

With that said, I can't deny that sometimes God does choose to come to the aid of maybe just one in a race allowing him/her to break free of physical limitations. One of my favorite stories in the Bible is the story of Elijah outrunning a chariot to Jezreel (a distance over a marathon...I'm pretty sure he ran faster than any of us elites are running today). Sometimes God does give supernatural strength. Knowing that God does move in this way is what makes going to the starting line such a thrilling experience for me. I believe with all my heart God can do something miraculous through me. While I cannot coerce God into moving in this way I still have childlike faith knowing it's possible, which I reflect in my running by being bold, taking chances and giving God an opportunity to do something amazing. However, I have found from my experience that oftentimes what I hear God telling me is, "My grace is sufficient for you" (2 Corinthians 12:9). God has always provided enough strength for me to do what He wants me to do on the race course. It doesn't mean I always win or do something miraculous but I always have enough to accomplish the purpose which God called me to race for.

I believe that the Bible is the best sports psychology book out there and that Jesus would have been an amazing athlete. My reasoning being that the Bible unlocks the perfect heart for athletes to compete from. The most important thing I can train is my heart. It is what drives the body. Christians should be able to compete with more freedom, less pressure and more joy. I have become better at being OK with whatever God has for me in a race knowing that at the end of the day, though I try to wrap my head around how God moves in sport, in the end, "As the heavens are higher than the earth, so are my ways higher than your ways and my thoughts than your thoughts" (Isaiah 55:9).

RT: Why do you have to be outspoken about your faith?

RH: Being a sports-crazy kid I always looked up to sports figures. At first it was Ken Griffey Jr., then Michael Jordan, then once I started running it changed to people like Jim Ryun and Eric Liddell. I wanted to know all about these guys and what it was that made them special at what they did. Now that I have a bit of notoriety I feel obligated to the fan to share all parts of me. I feel like it would be robbing those who are interested in my running to not share what it is that makes me tick and about the journey I am on. I realize that everyone might not agree with everything I believe in, and that's alright. I think we all need to extend the grace to one another to allow people to be who they are and say what makes them who they are.

RT: How does your running glorify God? Do you think he takes delight in your running the same way he delights in any other's craft, such as Kobe Bryant playing basketball or a professor teaching?

RH: I think that any time we are using our God-given gifts in the way God intended us to use them it glorifies God. So yeah, I would say God gets jazzed watching Kobe play basketball, just like we all do.

RT: If God wants you to be a world-class runner to glorify him, then why don't you always win? Why wouldn't God have wanted you to win the Olympics so that you could speak on the largest stage you'll ever have?

RH: I feel like my breakthrough moment in deciphering God's involvement in athletics came after the 2008 Olympic Marathon. I was feeling down for about a month after the race. I was trying to figure out why God didn't show up, why I didn't have my best stuff, and just why things went wrong for me from the outset of the Olympic preparations. A couple weeks after the race I heard a story that changed how I view God in athletics.

A church mission trip from a church that Sara and I follow very closely online and have developed a relationship with sent a group out to Kenya to do work in a non-sports related venture. On the last day of the trip their guide was very insistent that they must meet Sammy Wanjiru, who was putting his finishing touches on his training before leaving for Beijing.* They felt nervous about barging in on Sammy but the guide insisted. A long story short, they ended up praying that Sammy would experience God in a very real way in his race and I think every one, including Sammy, realized that his Olympic

---

* Wanjiru won the 2008 Olympic Marathon and the 2009 London and Chicago marathons.

record in those conditions was a God-filled run. To my understanding Sammy went back to Kenya and seriously pursued God.

After hearing of Sammy's story I began to understand that God being with me manifests itself in very different ways. It was easy for me to feel God's presence when it meant him taking me to new levels of physical performance but it took me years to learn to feel God's presence in my running even when I was struggling or just having an ordinary day. I don't believe God comes and goes as I once felt he did. I believe that as the Bible says, God is with those who are with him (Matthew 28:20; Deuteronomy 31:6; Isaiah 41:10), and this is my message. In a world where it is all about the guy on the top step of the podium and we are defined and define ourselves by the time on our watch, at the end of the day I am trying to spread the word that it ultimately isn't all about that. The sweetest part of life is that we can all have God. God is with those who are with him. It's our choice and a free invitation to everyone.

Having God with you doesn't always look like success in the world's eyes. Look at Paul—when he encountered God and started following Jesus, his life took a turn for the worse. He endured beatings, jail and ultimately death, yet God was undoubtedly with him. It says in the Bible that Mary was highly favored (Luke 1:28) yet she was with child apparently out of wedlock, which would alienate her from the Jewish community, and then was pretty much always on the run avoiding those who were trying to kill her son. She ultimately lost her son being crucified on a cross. Highly favored? That's not how I would define it. Yet what we don't read is what was going on in Mary's heart. Being highly favored, or winning as we might call it in the sports world, is an inner peace, joy, and freedom that comes from having God with us. It's not about the circumstances we are in but rather about the heart that we are able to have because of who is walking through all the circumstances of life with us.

With that said, sometimes God does make those who are with Him successful. The Bible says that "God was with Joseph, so he was successful in all he did" (Genesis 39:2). Not even selling him into slavery could keep him from being successful. I think the key here is not comparing ourselves to others. I know that I often struggle with looking around at other Christians, for example when Meb won the ING New York City Marathon, and not get jealous of what God had for him. The disciple Peter had the same problem when he was overhearing God's plan for the disciple John's life. Jesus responded, "If I want him to remain until I return what is that to you, you follow me" (John 21:22). Comparison is such a huge downfall for me and for, I believe, countless other athletes. When we lose our focus on just following Christ and we start looking to how God is moving in other people's lives it totally steals our joy, thankfulness and power.

RT: Along the same lines, wouldn't racing more often give you more opportunities to speak on a larger stage?

RH: Racing more often would only give me more opportunity to speak at a larger scale if I race well more often. Competing at the current marathon level is no walk in the park. It requires me to be totally invested, committed and most importantly, focused. Everyone is different but for me to get to the level I desire to get to it takes complete focus.

I love the focused life. It is what allowed me to become a professional runner in the first place. The high-school baseball coach tried to talk me into going out for the team my freshman year. If I would have taken him up on that I am certain I would have just been a mediocre baseball player and a good runner but not great at either. Jesus was focused on his mission to the point where he told one of his own disciples "get behind me Satan" (Matthew 16:23) when the disciple tried to persuade him from his mission. There is a lot of pressure to get distracted from my mission but I will not. I believe that God created me to run the marathon and run it well and I will not stop until he tells me it is time, and I will not be distracted unless he directs me to something different.

RT: Are you this good because you have worked and trained harder than everyone else, or because you are more blessed?

RH: Neither. I am what I am because of the grace of God. God's grace has allowed me to pick myself up out of the dirt time and time again. That grace is something we can all have. It obviously takes a lot of focus, discipline, humility, hard work and all those other things that make up great athletes but that is just who I am. We can all achieve a level of greatness when we are who we are meant to be to the fullest.

RT: When you run, have you ever felt God physically help you when running (a spurt of energy, strengthen a hurt muscle during a run, etc.)?

RH: God helps me physically every time I run. I run with my spirit. I don't think I am the only runner who would say they run with their spirit. I am sure that many of those who choose not to believe in God still believe they run with their spirit. I run with my spirit and I believe that God's spirit is inside me like it is available to all those who trust in Jesus. Not to say there aren't varying degrees of how much I experience God's spirit running inside me, because it does vary a lot depending on how intimate I am with God. I move sometimes, God doesn't. The Olympic Marathon Trials is probably the time when I felt the Holy Spirit the strongest in a race. It was an incredible experience that I believe we can all experience, even in the same race (meaning you might not win), depending on how desperate for God we are.

RT: Skeptics could very well say how convenient it is that at this point in your life God wants you to be a world-class runner. What is your response to that? Why wouldn't you more effectively be serving God by working to alleviate suffering here and now? Why isn't that a more direct form of ministry?

RH: Running is my ministry. I am using the body that God gave me to do what he wants me to do, including feeding and taking care of the poor. I knew from the very first time I went on an official run (15 miles around the lake in my hometown) that not only was God going to make me a world-class runner but that the purpose of that plan was to love and serve other people. When you look at the life of Jesus that is what he was all about. He said that those wanting to be the greatest should become a servant. It took a while for God to show me how I could use my running to serve others but we are really walking in it now after just launching the Hall Steps Foundation this fall with the goal of taking small steps toward the marathon goal of ending global poverty. It is both Sara's and my heart's desire to see the poor both domestically and internationally cared for and helped to their feet. I think the thing here is that it says in the Bible that God makes different vessels for different purposes so the vessel is not to look to its creator and say "Why have you created me this way?" (1 Corinthians 12:12-27).

The truth is that those who are not created to be the best in the world at something can experience the same level of satisfaction in daily living as the best guy or girl in the world if they are doing what they were created to do and they are not comparing themselves to others.

RT: What do you think about things like baseball players pointing to the sky when they hit a home run?

RH: I think it gets misinterpreted by a lot of fans. I see it as someone making a public statement of faith. I think they have every right to do so, living in this country of freedom. However, I think a lot of people see it, and perhaps some athletes mean it this way, as them saying God let them hit a home run. This interview is based around that very question: Did God allow him to hit the home run? My quick answer is God can do whatever he wants and perhaps he did supernaturally intervene at that moment or maybe he didn't. However, I would say that if that baseball player were operating very heavily out of the Holy Spirit in him then all of his actions would be God-directed.

RT: What would you say to someone who said that thinking you can divine God's working in your life is presumptuous?

RH: I don't feel like its presumptuous at all because it is not exclusive to just one person, ethnicity, gender, etc. Anyone who wants God can have him. It's their choice that I respectfully give them.

RT: Have you ever sensed that you've alienated other elites, such as Deena Kastor, who is Jewish, with your public faith?

RH: I used to be a lot more "preachy" in college and I think that hurt some of my friendships on the team. I have learned that my primary role as a Christian is to receive God's love and then to love others from that love. Now I am much more interested in hearing what others believe and why they believe it. I really enjoy talking about spiritual matters but if I sense my teammates don't feel like it or don't enjoy it, then I respect that. Deena and I get along very well.

RT: What would you say to a sponsor who asked you to tone down your outspokenness about faith? Have you ever sensed uneasiness from a sponsor about your faith espousals?

RH: I would hear my sponsors out and prayerfully consider what God would want me to do. I have never had this problem with Asics. They have been great in accepting and supporting my faith in the same way they accept and support all their athletes.

RT: Being an elite runner is an inherently selfish undertaking. How do you reconcile that with dying to Christ?

RH: I think you have this one backwards. It's not that we die to Christ. We die to sin and we are alive in Christ. "In the same way, count your-selves dead to sin but alive to God in Christ Jesus" (Romans 6:11). This is a huge misconception in Christianity that I am so adamant about clearing up. Being a Christian is not about dying to all our passions, desires, joys, and things we look forward to doing. It is about having them to the max. There is a transition period where maybe we do have to clean ourselves from unhealthy desires, passions, etc., but in the end we are supposed to have the most fulfilled life here on earth that we could dream of. We are supposed to be alive, fully alive, in Christ.

God wants me to enjoy my gift of running. He wants me to enjoy the disciplined lifestyle. He created me to be a focused individual that enjoys a disciplined, physically hard-working lifestyle. He created me this way. So when I do it, it feels right. It may appear to be selfish to some but I am doing what God designed me to do and the result will hopefully be exactly what God had in mind when he designed me.*

---

* Stephen Pyle, "Ryan Hall: The Faith Interview," *Running Times Magazine* © 2010 Running Times Magazine; Published under license from Rodale Inc.; Running Times Magazine is a trademark of Rodale Inc.; All rights reserved. Available online at runningtimes.com/Article.aspx?ArticleID=191 04&PageNum=1.

FRIDAY, MARCH 5

Morning workout
▶ 20-minute warm-up
▶ 12-mile tempo run
▶ 20-minute cooldown

Total miles: 18

Legs felt good. Still coughing up junk, but it is getting better. Ran down at Round Valley with Alistair for the first four miles, and then he pulled away. I pretty much caught up at eight miles, but he took off again for the last four. My goal was to keep my heart rate under 170 the whole way, which I pretty much did, plus or minus a couple of beats. Didn't run very fast. I averaged a 5:05 pace for the loop plus a couple miles down, but all things considered, with the cold and everything, it was a pretty solid day. This is exactly the way my workouts have been going all year. Solid runs but nothing exceptional compared to my training before other marathons.

It was a real challenge to see Alistair in front of me the whole way, to have him pull away, come back, and then pull away again the last couple miles. I felt like it was a good opportunity to focus on my own running—enjoying it and running my own rhythm even though I wasn't having a great day. I did a pretty good job of staying joyful out there and being happy for Alistair. I was just praying that God would continue to change my perspective, to give me the lens through which He sees the world, including the people I train with.

BLISTERS

Avoiding blisters can make a huge difference on race day. To keep my feet clean, I put Vaseline on them before long runs and marathons. Make sure you have plenty of space in your racing shoe at the starting line because by the end of the marathon your foot will be half a shoe size bigger. Trust me on this one.

Dealing with blisters when you have them is another matter altogether. I never remove the skin of the blister. I pop the blister with a sterile needle to drain it and then do my best to keep it clean. Removing the skin of the blister can cause lasting pain that can keep you sidelined.

If you deal with repeated blisters, check your shoes. Breaking in your shoes will also help to keep from getting blisters. I have found that with my racing shoes, I just do one short workout in them before the race and I am good to go, but you should find a system that works well for you. Socks are also key to keeping from getting blisters. I always use the thinnest socks I can find—Asics Lyte II Low Cut work perfectly for me.

Got strict orders from Coach to scratch the afternoon runs for the next couple of days until I get over the cold completely. Bummer! It's all good though. I need to kick this thing.

SATURDAY, MARCH 6

Morning workout
▶ Easy 75-minute run

Total miles: 11

Legs felt great. Not tired at all. I'm still coughing a lot, and I can still feel some fluid in my lungs, but I'm definitely improving rapidly. I expect that by the long run tomorrow I'll be functioning around 97 percent, and by Tuesday's workout this virus will be a distant memory. Such a gnarly cold. Man, it really wiped me out. I am thankful I didn't have to miss any hard workouts, only a little extra volume from three easy runs.

I watched "That's My King" (a powerful YouTube video of S.M. Lockridge describing Jesus) three times this morning. I love this video. It gets me fired up—not with my own confidence, but with the confidence of who God is and the power of what is inside of me.

On my run I was thinking about all that is in me and how I feel as if I am accessing very little of that. I want to experience more of God's power in my life, but I feel as if I'm being held back. I have so much pride and am so concerned with what others are thinking of me that I am inhibited when I worship in public. Things like this keep me from experiencing more of God because they take my focus off of God and put it on myself or others.

My greatest desire is to be more desperate for God. I am not exactly sure how to cultivate this. I have tried the disciplined life of reading a number of chapters each day or praying for a certain amount of time, but I find little fruit from that. I usually feel drained from the self-discipline instead of feeling recharged from my time in the Word. This is not to say I have never been recharged after disciplining myself to spend time with God, because I certainly have grown as a result of prayer, fellowship, worship, Bible reading, and so on. But I want more experiential time spent with God.

This afternoon I had an Asics photo shoot. Makeup, hair, and about 50 by 10-meter strides. All part of the job.

SUNDAY, MARCH 7

Morning workout
▶ Long run (2 hours, 15 minutes)
Total miles: 23.5

My legs and my body generally felt really good. I felt smooth and strong and didn't tighten up the way I did two weeks ago. Kept my heart rate around 155 or so for the first 90 minutes and then ran 10 by 90-second sprints with 90 seconds recovery. Got my heart rate up to 175 for the intervals, and then it usually came back down to 160 or so by the time I started the next one. Good run. Had fun despite some carnage going on out there with crazy surges from teammates. Good practice for Boston.

There is always someone feeling good. On Monday, Wednesday, and Thursday, Meb is moving along in the easy runs. On Tuesday it's Scotty and Alistair flying on the intervals. Friday it was Alistair on the tempo, and today it was Josh on the long run. Good opportunities to find a way to enjoy every run. Today I really did have a good time out there.

SIX
WEEKS TO BOSTON

MONDAY, MARCH 8

Morning workout
▶ Easy 75-minute run
Total miles: 11

Legs felt pretty good considering yesterday's distance and effort. Still hacking at the end of runs. This cold is lingering, but I'm trusting God to heal.

Afternoon workout
▶ Easy 35-minute run
▶ Hill sprints: 10 by 30 meters
Total miles: 5

Ran in a blizzard. Felt flat and tired this afternoon despite a two-hour nap. I hope I feel better tomorrow.

TUESDAY, MARCH 9

Morning workout
▶ 20-minute warm-up
▶ Intervals: 4:48 mile, 90 seconds rest, 2:50 kilometer, 600-meter jog—3 sets
▶ 20-minute cooldown
Total miles: 12

Didn't feel too snappy today. The cold is still in my system. I guess I should expect to feel a little flat after the quality long run Sunday. Ran by myself, which was good, so I could keep it under control. Surely this cold has almost run its course. It hit me pretty good.

SHOES

With five kids and a limited budget, my parents were always looking for bargains. When I started running, I picked up the cheapest pair of running shoes in Big 5 Sporting Goods and ran in them until the tread was completely worn off. I never forget that shoes are a luxury for most of the world's population, but professional runners need different types of shoes for each kind of run, so I have a pile of Asics just inside my front door.

Keeping my shoes fresh helps me avoid injuries and protect my legs from the pounding they receive on our asphalt and concrete roads. Barefoot running has made a stir in the past few years in America, but I always advise people to be cautious. I have seen people get injured from too much barefoot running. I do some occasional jogging barefoot on the grass after workouts for short periods to strengthen my feet but rarely for more than 20 minutes. I am all about going à la natural, but running on concrete and asphalt roads is not natural, nor is carrying around extra weight from not eating a totally natural diet. When we isolate one aspect of humanity's original lifestyle, things can go wrong.

When I choose a pair of shoes for a run, I consider terrain, pace, and distance. When I'm running easy, I want more cushion to allow my legs to recover, so I usually run in the Asics Gel Cumulus. When I am running at a medium-hard long run or uphill run, I go for a lightweight trainer—the Asics DS Trainer. I'm amazed at how much faster I can run in a slightly lighter shoe. When I am doing a long tempo run at marathon pace, I wear the Asics Hyper Speed II.

As I was cooling down and asking God for a good word, I felt Him reminding me of the story of Peter.

When Peter saw him, he asked, "Lord, what about him?"

Jesus answered, "If I want him to remain alive until I return, what is that to you? You must follow me." Because of this, the rumor spread among the brothers that this disciple would not die. But Jesus did not say that he would not die; he only said, "If I want him to remain alive until I return, what is that to you?"*

As I watched my teammates and what they were doing and how much faster they were running, I started getting caught in the comparison trap. As a result, I started to lose the joy in my spirit, the hope for my running, and the vision God has given me for Boston. God's reminder was timely because as I finished the cooldown and everyone was sharing their splits (which were much faster than mine), I started comparing their performance for the day with my own, which was by no means very special. However, I kept coming back to this verse and was encouraged to not look at what everyone around me is achieving, but to stay focused on Jesus and follow Him on my course.

As I rode in the back of the bus to Mammoth, I had some time to think about this buildup to Boston. It's been strange. None of my workouts have indicated that I am in incredible shape. However, I am still holding on to the vision God has given me for Boston—running effortlessly, laughing to myself at the goodness of God, singing the Hallelujah Chorus. It is definitely a walk of faith right now. Today I was struggling to run one mile at marathon pace. But running is such a crazy sport. I can be out there and I feel like a very average runner, and then maybe just a few days later, 4:50 feels like an easy pace.

Houston 2007 is still a mystery to me. I don't know if I will ever taste anything like that on earth again, but I have learned to go to the starting line believing anything is possible. He can make it happen again, and I believe He has encouraged me that it will happen again and has given me a vision for it. Right now I am walking by faith because my workouts have been nothing like the vision. But all I want is to get to the point where it's not even so much about the effortless performance, but about connecting with God out there. Lately I haven't been doing the best job of staying connected with God, both in my day-to-day life and in my running, but

---

* John 21:21-23 NIV

I have an increasing longing for a revival in my heart. He is so available to me and is waiting for me to go after Him, and that fills my heart with hope. I'm going after Him today.

Afternoon workout
▶ Easy 45-minute run

Total miles: 6.5

Legs felt okay. Crazy windy out there today and brutal cold. I'm ready for winter to be over.

WEDNESDAY, MARCH 10

Morning workout
▶ Easy 75-minute run

Total miles: 11

Legs felt good. Came off the workout really well. Ready for the uphill run tomorrow.

Afternoon workout
▶ Easy 45-minute run

Total miles: 6.5

Legs felt good. Found a nice afternoon run from the house that is exactly a 45-minute loop.

THURSDAY, MARCH 11

Morning workout
▶ 40-minute downhill run (5:20 pace, heart rate 140)
▶ 1-hour uphill run (sub-6:30 pace, heart rate 170, 4700 feet to 6700 feet)
▶ 10-minute cooldown

Total miles: 17

Legs felt much better today. It was the first day since two weeks ago when I first got the cold that I could really push. I ran faster on the uphill section than I did two weeks ago for the three 20-minute segments. Excited about how I am coming around. It is definitely easier to have fun when I'm feeling good.

Afternoon workout
▶ 25 minute warm-up
▶ Sprints: 6 by 150 meters
▶ 5-minute cooldown

Total miles: 7

Legs felt good on the warm-up, but after the first couple of strides, I was convinced that the 150s were long. They weren't. It was really good to recognize how my legs get so used to finding a comfortable rhythm doing marathon work. I need to break out of that from time to time and sprint hard. Was able to run some strides at a sub-4-minute-mile pace at the end. A lot of good running today!

FRIDAY, MARCH 12

Morning workout
▶ Easy 75-minute run

Total miles: 11

I felt good on the run. Excited for the marathon simulation tomorrow.

Afternoon workout
▶ 48-minute run

Total miles: 6.5

Brutal wind and snowstorm. I was practically walking at points when I was going straight into the wind. Still, despite it all, my legs felt good. Tomorrow's run should be a good one.

SATURDAY, MARCH 13

Morning workout
▶ 10 miles at 5:50 pace
▶ 10 miles at 5:06 pace
▶ 2-mile cooldown

Total miles: 22

Started at the camp at Round Valley (a mile above Boundary Road). My legs felt pretty good, but I didn't have as much pop as I thought I would have. With the downhill and the wind at my back the first couple of miles, I thought I was really going to roll, but I wasn't going that fast (4:47). I think I was a little tired from the uphill run a couple of days ago and the two hours of easy running yesterday.

I think I'm going to back off the volume on the easy days and try to hit the workouts a little harder. I know the wheels are there and will come out when I am rested, but with the workouts Coach sent me for my last two weeks up here in Mammoth, I am going to need to recover more on the easy days.

Still walking by faith. I know, I know, I know that something special is in this body. It just isn't showing itself yet. However, I am getting better at enjoying running even when I am not flying, making the most out of whatever I have on a given day. It helps a lot having the heart-rate monitor on. Today I was running up the hill from mile four to mile six against the wind and felt like I was walking. I was able to manage only 5:45 and 5:25 for those two miles, but with the heart-rate monitor on, I could see that I was putting out the right amount of effort. I ran the first 10 miles at 150 BPM and the second half at 170 BPM.

CLOTHING

Dressing properly for the conditions can make a big difference in the quality of a run. I have often dressed poorly and suffered through some long, miserable runs.

When I am heading out the door, I check the outdoor thermometer. I bring various layers so I can take clothes off as I go, especially in the winter. I start my runs feeling a little chilled because I know that five minutes into the run I will warm up and be ready to shed some layers. The best way for me to stay warm on really chilly mornings is to keep my extremities warm with thick socks, a thick beanie, and mittens rather than gloves.

In warm-weather running, a white hat and my Oakley sunglasses keep my face relaxed and prevent sun-induced headaches. I wear the lightest socks I can find to keep my feet from overheating on the hot pavement.

Patience is such a big part of distance running. I need to let the training come to me and not try to force it to come out. The times should just flow out of me without having to dig deep into the well every day. I am doing a good job of not going to the well. Being patient is difficult though. A little more than five weeks to go now. I can count the number of hard workouts left on my hands. I realize that I may never hit a great workout before Boston, but I know that when I back off and my legs and body come back to me, something special will come out. The only thing I can do to mess it up is to not rest enough in those last three weeks.

SUNDAY, MARCH 14

Morning workout
▶ Easy 90-minute run

Total miles: 13

Just the dogs and me out there today. Beautiful, blue sky. Had the earphones on and was singing praise to God, which is so freeing. This is my sanctuary. Sometimes, being alone out in the wilderness, listening to and singing praise music, I enjoy the best times of worship. They revitalize my spirit and my soul.

I didn't feel particularly good or bad today physically. Certainly not too beat up from the workout yesterday, which is good. I think I am always trying to find ways to push harder and harder, but sometimes my body protects me by not allowing me to go to the well. I can only go deep when I am rested.

FIVE
WEEKS TO BOSTON

MONDAY, MARCH 15

Morning workout
▶ Easy 73-minute run

Total miles: 11

Ran around town on the roads with Deena, Amy, Alistair, and Jon. Legs felt decent. A nice morning around town, nothing too exciting to report. Sometimes the beauty of a run is in its simplicity.

Afternoon workout
▶ Easy 35-minute run
▶ Strides: 8 by 60 meters
▶ Drills

Total miles: 7

It was so nice this afternoon. I walked out with two shirts and full tights and had to strip down to half tights, a long-sleeved shirt, and no hat for the run. Legs felt a lot better this afternoon after hitting up a two-hour nap.

When I was doing my strides, I was considering my fitness and how small the difference is between my threshold pace and my interval pace. Some coaches would see this as a flaw, but I see it as a sign that my marathon fitness is going through the roof. Last week I struggled to run 4:50 for some of my miles during an interval workout, yet I was able to average pretty close to 5:00 a mile for my ten-mile tempo after ten miles medium-hard and a very big day just two days before that. It is a good sign to be only 15 seconds a mile slower than interval pace. When my legs freshen up and I'm able to run somewhere around 4:30 pace for a mile at a time, my strength will also follow suit and come down to 4:45 pace when I put it all together. Of course, it doesn't always translate this nicely or evenly, but sometimes it does. I need to remember when working out on tired legs that I am really fit even if the watch doesn't say so.

TUESDAY, MARCH 16

Morning workout
- ▶ 20-minute warm-up with drills and strides
- ▶ Intervals: 1200 at 3:30, 2 minutes rest, 1200 at 3:28 (middle 400 in 66)—4 sets
- ▶ 20-minute cooldown

Total miles: 12

"Blessed is the man who trusts in the LORD."* This verse ran through my head and a broad smile worked its way across my warm bearded face while I completed my warm-up drills before today's workout. I was smiling not only because my legs were feeling more and more like their old selves but also because I could feel my heart being released from the heaviness I've been carrying around.

My heaviness is coming from the self-induced pressure to win Boston. My newfound freedom comes from trusting in God and enjoying His presence. In His presence nothing else matters, not even winning Boston. My heart was at peace, and my face was showing it. It felt great to trust God. It is such a simple thing to do, yet it slips away so easily as I begin to focus on performance. But the moment I put my trust in God, my burden is lifted and my yoke is light. Blessed is the man who trusts in the Lord!

The workout went well today—certainly a lot better than last week. Sixty-six seconds for 400 meters still doesn't feel like butter, but I can tell some pop is returning to my legs compared to last week, when a 4:50 mile took a bit of effort. I am happy with how things are progressing. I have a day

---

* Jeremiah 17:7

less than five weeks till the Boston Marathon, which can seem like a short time, but I'm actually only halfway through my buildup to Boston. The best is yet to come.

ENERGY FOOD

Many people run to lose weight, but I maintain a delicate balance of staying lean while still fueling myself well. I often remind myself when I am training hard that yesterday's energy in equals today's energy out.

The body can absorb only so much in one sitting. I eat often (every two hours), choosing from fruits, veggies, and a balance of carbs, protein, and fat. I learned a lot from working with nutritionist Dr. Clyde Wilson from Stanford.

Dr. Clyde taught me that when carbo-loading, my body can store only about 400 extra calories from loading the day before, so there is no point in adding more than this amount to my typical intake. I also learned to spread the load over the two or three days before a race.

Living and training at altitude requires me to closely monitor my iron levels. I avoid calcium and wheat in conjunction with the iron-rich foods because they hinder the absorption of iron.

I also make sure I get enough omega-3 fatty acids. Instead of supplements, every day I add a tablespoon of ground flaxseed to my cereal or eat some sardines, salmon, or walnuts. I also focus on foods that are naturally high in antioxidants, such as green tea, berries, cinnamon, and other antioxidant-rich foods. Great recovery foods include pineapple, whey protein, and juice.

I try to avoid consuming a lot of sugar, but I still include it in my coffee, and like to end my meals with the darkest chocolate I can find (in moderation, of course). I eat lots of healthy rice and grains, as these provide the ready fuel I need. The healthier I eat, the more I crave such foods and enjoy giving my body high-quality fuel. I like to focus on what I *can* eat, not on all the things I am choosing not to eat. When I do make an occasional indulgence, I realize I don't really miss the highly processed and refined foods that fill our supermarkets today.

Coach had a good word for the team at the end of our workout when we were shooting the breeze. He was talking about not comparing workouts or buildups to previous ones. He said that if you watch today's sunrise thinking of yesterday's sunset, you missed the beauty of today's sunrise. That's a good word!

I do this all the time. I am always putting today's workouts next to my best workouts and comparing the two. I strongly believe this severely limits my ability to break through and get the most out of myself. When I constantly compare my workouts, I can't be excited about where I am currently. I have been running for so many years, rarely will I run my best workout ever. I have to look at each workout as a stepping-stone to getting into my best shape ever. But I can't maintain this perspective when I'm down on myself simply because I'm not in the best shape of my life. I have to be able to get the positive out of the workout and build momentum from it. That mental momentum is nearly as important as the physical buildup.

Not comparing workouts is one of the keys to breaking through to enjoying running and enjoying every day on the road—regardless of whether a new personal best comes.

Afternoon workout
▶ Easy 38-minute run

Total miles: 5

Sara finally returned from Doha, Qatar, after being gone for a long two weeks. It's so good to have her home. We ran together this morning, and after being home alone for so long with no one but the dogs to talk to, I jabbered away quite a bit on our run, which isn't my usual style.

Legs felt really good. I came off the workout well.

WEDNESDAY, MARCH 17

Morning workout
▶ Easy run (1 hour, 45 minutes)

Total miles: 16

Had such a great run today! I went down to Round Valley with Sara so she could do a photo shoot with *Runner's World*. I remembered a trail there that I hadn't run since 2005, when we first moved to Mammoth—Lower Rock Creek Trail. After spending a lot of time on the road this winter, I was in heaven running on a single track trail that winds along a small creek.

Felt like this run was meant to be—just me running through the forest. Any heaviness I was carrying melted away and the peace of God filled me as the warm wind blew through my hair and I enjoyed God's creation. I hardly looked at my watch to see when I had to turn around. These moments are why I will always run. I felt good, lost track of time, and just communed with God and His creation. I could feel my heart filling up.

I have a ton of respect for people who don't get to run in scenic locations. I can enjoy the simple act of running regardless of where I am, but it is definitely a lot easier on trails like Lower Rock Creek. I strongly believe that we can experience the same peace of God that I experienced today anywhere and anytime, but certain situations make achieving that peace a lot easier. The ultimate goal is to operate with this peace 24/7. If I am running on the hectic streets of Boston and want to enter into this peace of God, all I have to do is close my eyes, imagine myself back on Lower Rock Creek, and remember the sensation I felt today.

THURSDAY, MARCH 18

Morning workout
▶ Easy 75-minute run

Total miles: 10

My legs felt really good today, but I took it easy because I have a big run coming up tomorrow. No need to air it out yet. Legs are feeling cleaner (less adhesions and tightness) and lighter than they have felt in a long time. I can't help but feel something special is in there. I know it. It is brewing in me. I feel the same way I felt before London 2008 and Houston 2007. There I go, remembering yesterday's sunrise and missing today's sunrise! It is so easy to slip back into comparing myself to previous buildups. The important thing is that I feel really good.

Afternoon workout
▶ Easy 35-minute run

Total miles: 5

Moved along a bit...I couldn't help myself. Ran the afternoon loop 90 seconds faster than I have during this buildup. Legs felt good this afternoon. Totally clean and full of run, as I like to say. Felt like I was floating along. Coming along nicely. Tomorrow should be good!

FRIDAY, MARCH 19

Morning workout
▶ 20-minute warm-up with drills and strides
▶ 15-mile tempo run at 5:02 pace
▶ 20-minute cooldown

Total miles: 20.5

Started five miles north of Green Church Road, turned on to Green

Church Road and ran to the nine-mile mark, and turned around and finished at the eight-mile mark to avoid a brutal hill farther out the road. Big day this morning. The first of my-15 mile tempo runs is usually nothing to write home about...oops, there I go comparing. If you would have told me I would manage to run 5:02 pace before the run I would have been quite happy, yet somehow by the end of the tempo run I found myself discouraged with my fitness. It all goes back to comparing this workout to my all-time best. I should be thrilled that I am moving forward, had my best tempo run of the buildup, and felt good, but considering I was ripping off 12-mile tempo runs at 4:50 pace before London, today feels less than impressive.

ELECTROLYTE REPLACEMENT DRINKS

I commonly use electrolyte drinks in my workouts to help replace electrolytes I lose through sweat if I am running more than 45 minutes in extreme heat.

In races, elite marathoners get their own precisely measured bottles every 5k, so I practice drinking between four and eight ounces at the same interval in practice. The first bottles are pretty diluted. They peak in strength near halfway in the marathon, and they are more diluted again near the finish.

Replacing all the water and electrolytes I lose during the run would be impossible. Bodies naturally lose water weight as the race progresses. The idea is to replace only what the body will effectively absorb. The general consensus is that in a marathon, the body can only absorb roughly 200 calories an hour without causing stomach distress. So I take gels periodically for quick energy hits that my body responds to well.

The key is to do in practice exactly what you will do on race day. Find out what electrolyte beverage will be served on the course and use this beverage in the last months leading up to the event. Practice with the same gels that are provided on the course or plan to bring your own. If you want to dilute your first couple of drinks, grab one cup of electrolyte drink and a cup of water to drink with it. A good general practice is to take in an electrolyte beverage every 20 minutes—more often in hot weather.

Sometimes I feel so weighed down by the need to hit times. Even before the warm-up, I could feel myself getting nervous about managing a five-minute pace. Really though, that pace is totally arbitrary. What really matters is running the right effort, having fun, and seeing how the workout fits into the bigger picture of training. Those things are easier said than done, of course. I realized today that I still have an attitude that needs adjusting before I hit the starting line in Hopkington. I need to stop comparing myself to myself, stop seeing myself in light of my best performance ever, and simply enjoy running and connecting to God. I am getting closer and getting better at handling days like today, when I have a solid run but certainly not my best ever. I know that running can be such a great experience every time out if my perspective is right heading into workouts. I need to let go of the times! This would be a huge breakthrough for me.

Afternoon workout
▶ Easy 35-minute run
Total miles: 5.5

Legs felt stiff when I first started, but then they opened up nicely and actually I moved along a bit on the back half. There is still juice in these legs. Had a bit of a mental breakthrough this afternoon. I was stretching and had that same vision I've had for myself over and over again. I see myself running totally free from worry, expectation, heaviness, pride...running with pure joy and connection with God. Something clicked as I pictured this, and I know that this vision will become a reality one day as long as I keep going after it. I need to continue to find ways to take the pressure off and just enjoy the simple act of running. I'm getting there. I'm just slow.

SATURDAY, MARCH 20

Morning workout
▶ Easy 60-minute run
Total miles: 9

First day of spring! Yeah buddy! Legs felt better than I was expecting. Ran with Sara on the only open dirt road in Mammoth.

Afternoon workout
▶ Easy 35-minute run
Total miles: 5.5

Legs felt surprisingly good. It's amazing how the body learns to recover after hard days.

SUNDAY, MARCH 21

Morning workout
▶ Long run (2 hours, 30 minutes)
Total miles: 26.53

I came through the marathon in 2:27:55. Not a personal best, but I'll take it for practice. Legs felt really good today. Felt very easy going the whole way. Included some sprints. Felt much smoother than the long run two weeks ago. About 2:05 into the run, I started to get the familiar right hip tightness. With my experience with the pain in the NYC Marathon, I know I can run through it.

Ran with Meb at a chill pace for the first 45 minutes. Starting to see some evidence of that special stuff I have been feeling inside. Hit a series of five-minute miles that felt real chill. Not bad considering what I did two days ago. I think dialing in my nutrition has been a big help. Working with a nutritionist has not only helped physically—feeling well-fueled with more energy throughout the day—but also assures me that I'm eating the right way. I haven't had many huge changes, but the small changes have made a big difference.

Today was beautiful and warm. I even got to run with my shirt off for the last hour. It probably wasn't a pretty sight for everyone else considering how white I am right now, but it sure felt good to me! Winter makes the spring feel brighter and warmer.

I got rocked in church tonight. God continues to encourage me and give me visions for my running. As I worshipped, I felt a little guilty because I was also thinking about running, but then I remembered that "there is now no condemnation for those who are in Christ Jesus"* and that I should allow God to speak to me about my passions. God was giving me visions for Boston. I had chills as I felt myself moving over the Boston course. I know God has something special waiting for me there.

---

* Romans 8:1

FOUR
WEEKS TO BOSTON

MONDAY, MARCH 22

Morning workout
▶ Easy 70-minute run

Total miles: 10

Legs felt a little tight when I started, but after the first 20 minutes, they loosened up and I felt much better. Just Sara, me, and the dogs today. Beautiful sunny morning. The weather the last couple weeks has been amazing. Spring is here!

Afternoon workout
▶ Easy 35-minute run

Total miles: 5

Legs felt surprisingly good this afternoon.

TUESDAY, MARCH 23

Morning workout
▶ 20-minute warm-up with drills and strides
▶ Intervals: 1 mile in 4:40 and 1k in 2:50—3 sets
▶ 20-minute cooldown

Total miles: 12

Legs didn't have a ton of pop in them, but I still had a good workout considering the high volume I am at. My quads felt tired. I didn't have a lot of drive in my legs, but I was able to practice turning it over even on slightly tired legs. Usually when I am running hard and trying to pick it up, I just keep driving my legs and arms without changing my mechanics. But Sunday's long run included a crazy steep hill coming out of the gorge at about mile 18. It's only about half a mile long but has a 12 percent grade. On that hill, and again today, I increased my turnover (as if I were running on hot coals) and even lowered my knee drive. These short strides feel weird when I first start them, and I don't feel as if I'm running fast, but they actually help me run faster and more efficiently.

HYDRATION SYSTEMS

When I was preparing for the 2008 Beijing Olympic Marathon, I knew that hydration was going to be a key factor. To help me prepare for the unique challenge of running in hot and humid conditions, Steve, my older brother, rode a bike next to me, pacing me and providing fluid support. He was a huge asset to me during this time.

The best hydration system is to have someone on a bike giving you fluid every 20 minutes on your runs lasting an hour or more, but this is not possible for everyone. Many great hydration products are available—belts, packs, vests, and straps for handheld bottles. When I'm on my own, I stash bottles along the route every three miles.

I'm reminded that my fastest times in practice are not as important as what I am able to do in a workout with tired legs. Even though my workout times haven't been very impressive, I have run all of them on tired legs and am continuing to improve. This is the first week of cutting back to my normal volume for easy runs during marathon training. Running two hours a day was keeping my legs pretty tired. Now, in the last month of training, I can cut that back and let some of the pop come back into my legs. Instead of doing 45-minute afternoon runs, I will only run 30 to 35 minutes. And instead of doing 75-minute morning runs, I will more likely run 60 minutes. Even though I have some big, tough workouts this week, I expect to start feeling faster because I'm running shorter easy runs.

Afternoon workout

▶ Easy 45-minute run

Total miles: 6.5

Legs felt pretty good. Quads still felt dead. Glad to have a massage to work them out.

WEDNESDAY, MARCH 24

Morning workout

▶ Easy 60-minute run

Total miles: 8.5

Legs felt good today. Ran at Tom's Place on dirt and snow.* Typical springtime run. Had fun running with the team. I'm amazed that we are able to run easy runs together regardless of gender and event. Anna was the second-ranked 800-meter runner in the world last year, and Deena, Meb, and I are marathoners, yet we all run together on easy days. The middle-distance crew usually runs about 75 percent of the mileage we do.

Afternoon workout

▶ Easy 35-minute run
▶ Sprint drills

Total miles: 5

Legs felt good. My last uphill run tomorrow should be fun. Still sleeping a ton. Every easy day, I am taking two-hour naps, which is about 30 minutes longer than usual. That tells me my body is still pretty tired.

---

* Tom's Place is a small town about 20 minutes south of Mammoth.

THURSDAY, MARCH 25

Morning workout

▶ 7.6-mile downhill
▶ 7.4-mile climb from 4500 feet to 7000 feet
▶ 6-mile downhill

Total miles: 21

Ran down from Swall Meadows and then up and back down Power Poles.*
Kind of a blah day. Flying somewhat out of control down the first downhill section never feels that great regardless of how I feel going into the
workout. I was all fired up to better my time from two weeks ago, but I
hit a nasty headwind. Running into any headwind is a test of patience,
but running uphill into a steady headwind will test your sanity. I felt as if
I were standing still at points. Then after 50 trying minutes, I got to flip
and run downhill with the wind, which you'd think would be fun, but the
grade was so steep that my legs felt as if they were being beaten with a baseball bat. It seemed like with every step I could feel something new bothering me. First my hip, then up high in my hamstrings, then my quads,
and then my calves. I was running 4:45 miles, but I couldn't even take joy
in that. I found myself thinking, *Here I am, bombing downhill with a tailwind, and I can barely manage marathon pace.* However, once I thought
about it, I realized that running down a steep grade is sometimes harder
than running on the flat—at least on the legs.

Afternoon workout

▶ Hour massage
▶ 20 minutes of therapeutic pool work
▶ Hour stretch from Coach. No run!

---

* A maintenance road that is lined with power poles and that we often use for uphill runs.

FRIDAY, MARCH 26

Morning workout
▶ Easy 60-minute run
Total miles: 8

Legs felt tired. Woke up this morning sore. Quads, calves, and hips are a mess. Took it easy.

Afternoon workout
▶ Easy 35-minute run
Total miles: 5

Legs felt a lot better this afternoon after a long nap. Still not poppy though.

SATURDAY, MARCH 27

Morning workout
▶ Easy 50-minute run
Total miles: 7.5

Ran with Alistair and Luke, faster than I would have gone on my own.* Last run on Straight Road. I'm thankful for the dirt at high altitude, but I'm not going to miss this road. Last full day in Mammoth before heading to Boston.

Afternoon workout
▶ Easy 35-minute run
Total miles: 5

My legs felt a lot better, and I thought I was moving along, but my Garmin disagreed. I found out my afternoon loop is a mile shorter than I

---

* Luke Gunn is the 2009 National 3000 steeplechase champion.

thought—only 4.62 miles—so I've been running slower on my easy days than I thought. I had to remind myself that some world-class runners jog ten-minute miles on their easy days. I think this is a very individual thing and shouldn't be forced. A six-minute pace is the gold standard for easy running among elite distance runners, but the real gold standard is paying attention to your body and recovering.

SUNDAY, MARCH 28

Morning workout
▶ Marathon simulation

Total miles: 24

I am flying to Los Angeles, looking over the white mountains that are my home. I have had a great training stint up here. I am thankful to get to train in this beautiful place. Even though I still have yet to really pop a workout, I am feeling really good heading into Boston. I've trained and prepared my heart for what lies ahead, and that is the most important thing I can do. I've been dropped by everyone on the team and still been able to find joy. I've felt terrible on easy runs. I've run through upset stomachs. I've run a really poor half-marathon, limping into the finish in disappointment. I've disrupted my routine with travel more than usual. I've opened my mind to the benefits of training at sea level. I've had to seek help to get long-standing adhesions and tightness worked out of my body. I've learned how to take care of my body on my own and do my own therapy. But perhaps the most important lesson I have learned and continue to learn is to be free from gauging my value by my performances and to connect with God.

ALL ABOUT EQUIPMENT

Running can be as simple or complex as you want it to be. Here are some of my favorite pieces of equipment:

My Garmin Forerunner 110 GPS watch has revolutionized my ability to train when traveling. I can go anywhere in the world and keep track of my pace, splits, and distance. Ten years ago, GPS watches looked like giant computers on your wrist. Not anymore. The Garmin Forerunner 110 is light and small, but it does everything you need a GPS watch to do. If you travel a lot, as I do, I strongly recommend it.

I always thought sunglasses were a matter of style rather than function, but my thoughts have certainly changed after training with my Oakley sunglasses. I can attest to their performance-enhancing functionality. The lenses are hydrophobic (they repel liquids, such as sweat and beverages), they transition (darker in the sun, lighter in the shade), and the new Oakley Jawbones are even breathable, keeping the lenses from fogging up. Staying relaxed is one of the most effective ways to enhance performance.

Asics Chafe Free can make the difference between being stranded on the side of the road with nasty chafing and blisters, or running pain free to the finish line, so I lube up before my long runs and tempo runs. Chafing and blisters are among the most easily prevented injuries in running. I also use band-aids for my nipples because they can take a beating in certain conditions. After setting the American record in the half-marathon, my nipples were the most painful part of my body. Again, this is easily preventable with some simple equipment.

Music is a hot topic for runners. Elite athletes are not allowed to use personal music devices in races, but I train with mine from time to time. They are so small and lightweight, they certainly don't hinder my range of motion and can serve as a good running partner. I listen to the audio Bible, podcasts, worship music, or my favorite dance music. I also like using music to put me into the right spirit before I head to the starting line.

This morning in Round Valley I ran ten miles at moderate effort in 57:45 (5:46 pace) and ran the next 12 miles in 1:00:30 (5:02 pace). This was my best tempo run of the year. My legs felt good today. As I began the tempo portion (slightly downhill and with the wind at my back), I looked at my Garmin in disbelief as it projected my first mile time to be in the 4:30s. It felt so smooth and effortless. I had to hit the breaks to ensure I didn't run too fast because my goal for the tempo run was 5:10 pace. I came through the mile in 4:48 and felt as smooth as butter. But as the terrain flattened and the wind shifted, my pace returned to about five minutes, which is what I have become accustomed to during this buildup. But I was able to break through emotionally, have fun, and run with the right amount of effort.

When I was hitting some slow miles out there, I was able to relax more and just enjoy being out there. I kept telling myself that if I'm not able to enjoy myself, I am running too hard. This may sound counterintuitive, but when I am having fun, I can push myself way harder than when I am just out there focusing on pushing. Enjoyment is a big part of unlocking our hidden potential. I am sure of it.

I am also learning to be thankful for each day's run regardless of how slow or fast it is, and I'm starting to catch myself when I begin to compare today's run to other buildups or other people. Comparisons keep me from realizing my potential. I am also getting better at connecting with God while I run, realizing that He loves to watch me run and is always with me. Being increasingly aware of His presence makes whatever I am doing sweeter and sweeter.

Week Twelve

THREE
WEEKS TO BOSTON

MONDAY, MARCH 29

Morning workout
▶ Easy 60-minute run

Total miles: 8

Ran from our airport hotel in Los Angeles down to the beach. It was a beautiful warm morning. My legs felt pretty good considering the hard work I did yesterday. I couldn't help but feel good with a fresh pair of shoes and my first run at sea level in nearly two months. I like to call it the third-lung effect. With the exception of Phoenix in January, I almost always feel like I have a third lung the first day down at sea level. When I was in the airport last night, I could feel the difference just walking. I wonder if babies feel that way when they take in that first deep breath. I feel as if I've been operating at 70 percent lung capacity while at altitude. It is a great feeling as a runner—my rib cage seemed to expand overnight.

Feeling this good, I have to make sure I keep taking it easy. Sara and I had a great time just talking and laughing as we goofed off sprinting away from each other randomly. For the next three weeks, I need to focus on resting. When I was a high-school senior, even though I didn't feel overtrained, I went into my state qualifying track meets running very poorly. My dad made me take it really, really easy for a couple of weeks. Resting that much felt all wrong, but it was all I could do because I had tried the alternative—training harder. With the added rest, nothing changed overnight, but I went from a fried, really hard 4:14 mile one week to a smooth 4:10 the next week and a 4:05 the following week. By the end of three weeks of doing next to nothing, I felt great and ran a 4:02, which was a state record at the time. The fourth week, I ran my 1500 PR—3:42.7. I would have never rested if it were left up to me, but I trusted my dad and took it easy.

I'm feeling similar in regard to the next three weeks, except that I haven't overtrained. The goal is to rest as much as possible. We have shortened some of my workouts and broken up my last long tempo. The key will be to take the edge off the workouts. The temptation will be to prove my fitness to myself, but that's not what my body needs. My body needs to let that special feeling that I've had during this buildup brew in me until race day. I don't want to let it out during the next three weeks. I can already feel that temptation, so I think I will need to set some pace guidelines to ensure I don't run my race in practice. If it brews for the next three weeks, I believe I will have an experience very similar to my senior year in high school. The hard work has been done, and now it's time to rest.

This afternoon we fly to Boston, where we'll be training until the race!

TUESDAY, MARCH 30

Morning workout
▶ 20-minute warm-up with drills and strides
▶ Intervals: 6 by 1200 in 3:30 with 400 float jogs
▶ 20-minute cooldown

Total miles: 16

Great to be back on the Boston course today. I love this course. It has so much character. It reminds me of many of the mountains I have run up. There are lots of challenges along the way, which make for an adventure. The finish is the icing on the cake.

Didn't feel particularly poppy today. My legs felt a little like Jell-O because of the travel yesterday. Or maybe it was just two-day onset fatigue from the marathon simulation. I guess it could have also been the intense cold headwind and the downpour. Regardless, my times were nothing to write home about, but it isn't about that anyway. Had fun out there and worked the course hard from miles 14.5 to 20.5. Good to see those hills in Newton again and, more importantly, that sixteenth mile, which is so underestimated.

Afternoon workout

▶ Easy 30-minute run

Total miles: 4

Legs felt decent after getting some ART from Dr. Green (a local practitioner). Tried to find some cool trails around our new home base in Waltham but ended up running up steep trails in another cold downpour. Welcome to Boston!

WEDNESDAY, MARCH 31

Morning workout

▶ 70-minute run

Total miles: 10

Ran in and around Harvard while Sara did a workout on the track. My legs, or rather my entire body, felt like trash. Felt the travel even more today than yesterday. Still had a nice run around the river. Took it easy and tried to enjoy myself, but it is tough when I feel this way.

I'm already starting to overanalyze how I am feeling. This typically happens before all my big races, and I've learned to manage it. I seem to think my legs should feel remarkably great on every run now that I'm tapering, whereas when I am training hard, I'm not too concerned with how my legs feel. During the buildup, I just train hard, accept that I will be tired after hard days, and expect to feel much better in the workouts. But the mentality begins to shift in the last few weeks leading up to major races. I can see this more objectively in some of my teammates. I know they are fit, and it doesn't matter how they feel on a particular day right before a race because their fitness level will not change. However, when I am the one getting close to that big race, managing these feelings is difficult.

I keep reminding myself that I didn't feel all that spectacular on my easy runs leading up to London, and I still ran 2:06. I wish I could put the issue to rest once and for all, but this isn't usually how it works. I usually put it to rest, but it resurfaces, so I have to constantly keep myself in check.

RUNNING IN GROUPS AND RUNNING ALONE

I am blessed to be a part of the Mammoth Track Club. I can hardly imagine running at a high level without being a part of a training group. Additionally, sharing the day-to-day experience of running with others is what running is all about.

Our team meets six days a week, twice a day, and yet we still find excuses to get together and have parties. Though we meet together every day, we don't run every step together. We all have unique and varied plans. I like to do many of my workouts on my own to ensure I am not racing in practice or getting dragged along faster than I should go. But doing a workout with a teammate is sometimes very helpful and enjoyable.

Most of the negative effects of running with a team have to do with pride and comparisons. During my first two years at Stanford, I fell into the trap of comparing myself to others and proving to myself and everyone else what kind of shape I was in. Working that hard on every run resulted in gradual overtraining. When I set my pride aside and ran with the group at my proper effort level, I finally broke through and led my team to an NCAA Division I Cross Country team title. Today, I set my pride aside on the easy days and often run slower than many of the women on our team because that is what is right for me on that particular day.

Afternoon workout
▶ Easy 30-minute run with drills

Total miles: 4

Felt way better than this morning. Found some decent trails near the track where Sara did her afternoon sprints.

THURSDAY, APRIL 1

Morning workout
▶ 70-minute run

Total miles: 10

Started at Wellesley and ran out to the 15k mark of the Marathon course and back. Legs and body felt back to normal today. It's amazing how much the body can recover in a day. It helped to run the course backward and see it from different angles. Picked up a few things about subtle ups and downs. Can't believe April is here. Time goes by too fast.

Afternoon workout
▶ Easy 30-minute run with drills and strides

Total miles: 4

First run from our place in Waltham. It's about three miles from the Newton Hills and at the 17.5-mile mark on the course. Didn't find anywhere special to run, but the sun was out for the first time since we arrived here. What a beautiful afternoon. Its amazes me how much the sun can change the way a place looks. My last big, hard workout is tomorrow. Looking forward to it. Legs felt a lot better on the drills and strides.

FRIDAY, APRIL 2

Morning workout
▶ 20-minute warm-up
▶ 5 miles with 1-mile float—3 sets
▶ 20-minute cooldown

Total miles: 23 miles

Ran about 4:50 pace for the hard sessions and about 5:50 pace for the easy miles. Came through the first 17 miles of the course in 1:24:30 (4:58

pace). Legs felt strong. I am still not used to turning my legs over so fast. I felt as if I were flying the whole time but also felt able to push and push and push. Felt very strong—exactly where I want to be. I know the turnover will continue to improve as I rest and do more workouts at sea level.

Very pleased with how today went. To be able to run under a five-minute pace with a couple easy miles in there was very encouraging. This was a huge confidence booster for me. If I can keep it rolling at 4:50s the whole way on race day, I will be thrilled whether I win or lose. Of course, it's not about the time, but I love to run fast, and if the right day presents itself, I believe I could manage 4:50s on this course.

Though I've continually battled focusing too much on my running times, I think it's possible to have a healthy perspective on it. I have always lived at extremes, training really hard or not training at all, eating really healthy or eating nothing but junk, and so on. But today, running 4:50s out there, I was just loving the test. I think the key is not making time what it is ultimately all about. I need to adopt a more healthy perspective, accepting whatever times the day holds and being equally excited whether running 5:00 pace or 4:40 pace. Not comparing my times to my previous times or to anyone else's times is also important. If I can do this, I think I can still keep track of my times, be excited about running fast, and yet not let the watch determine whether or not a run was successful.

It was a beautiful, sunny day on the course. Kind of a weird crosswind today. Still have yet to experience a tailwind. I am beginning to question whether it exists, though I've been told it does more than 50 percent of the time. Great to start from the beginning and get a sense of what it is like to run hard over those early miles. But most importantly, I had fun out there, and am getting excited to race!

I accidently drank my recovery protein shake instead of my caffeinated gel halfway into my workout, but I didn't even realize it until after the workout was complete. Oops. Hope that doesn't happen on race day.

Legs felt pretty beaten up afterward. Glad I am taking a couple of easy days before my last long run before the race. Getting a massage today as well.

RUNNING LOGS

When I first started running, I kept a very detailed training log. My dad still has my high-school journals and often referred back to them when he coached our local high-school cross-country team to numerous state titles. I was adamant about keeping my log up-to-date. I loved to record my workouts and add up my mileage at the end of the week. I bolstered my confidence before races by seeing how far my workouts had progressed and how much work I had done.

In college I grew tired of keeping a log. I also came to the realization that keeping a log showed I had worked harder than everyone else didn't necessarily mean I would run faster. It was the beginning of the realization that as in life, so in training: Sometimes less is more. I also realized that my intensely passionate personality easily became obsessive about running. Keeping a detailed training log was adding to my struggle with becoming overly focused on my running goals.

I didn't return to a training log until I began this journal. My coach has e-mailed me workouts on spreadsheets since 2005, and I have saved them all, but I rarely recorded my times. Sometimes I wish I could look back on a more detailed training log. Once I am all done with running, I will probably wish I had kept a better log, but right now, not keeping a log works best for me.

Keeping a detailed training log and recording my thoughts in a daily journal leading up to the 2010 Boston Marathon has been life changing. Writing is relaxing and deeply therapeutic, so this has been a powerfully positive tool in my life.

The best log is one that you enjoy and that is easy to use. There are many logs to choose from today, including online logs, spreadsheets, and even smartphone applications. When I was keeping my journal, I just opened up a Word document and started writing. If you are philosophical like me, perhaps writing in a journal will be better than plugging raw data into a traditional training log. Experiment and find what works for you. I do recommend writing in some way to remind yourself on a daily basis of your goals.

SATURDAY, APRIL 3

Morning workout
▶ Easy 45-minute run
Total miles: 6

My legs were definitely a little tired and beaten up from yesterday, but I enjoyed running in Salisbury, where Sara was running a low-key four-mile race as a tempo run. My legs eventually loosened up and actually were feeling good by the end.

Being at a road race with such a fun, happy-go-lucky atmosphere was refreshing. I enjoy environments where the perspective on running is so much more relaxed. The joy of the people who were there to take part in a fun running event with their friends was contagious. I'm grateful for their encouragement.

Afternoon workout
▶ Easy 40-minute run
Total miles: 6

Enjoyed a fun, adventurous afternoon at Hampton Beach, New Hampshire. I got a henna tattoo (wings on each of my ankles, which is the only tattoo I have entertained the idea of actually sporting), ate lobster and clams at a roadside restaurant, and took a nap on the beach.

Legs felt significantly better than this morning. Still some tightness, but that is to be expected.

SUNDAY, APRIL 4

Morning workout
▶ Easy 30-minute run

Total miles: 4.5

Easter Sunday! Ran around the streets of Harvard after church while Sara, her sister Amy, and Amy's boyfriend got us a table at a restaurant for brunch. Legs felt pretty good.

God encouraged me this morning. First, while reading a book called *Possessing Joy* by Steve Backlund, I came to a chapter called "Destination Disease." Steve writes about the trap of saying, "If I accomplish this, then I will be happy." If we are not happy now, we will not be happy when we reach our destination, whether that destination is winning the Boston Marathon, setting a personal best, winning an age group, or something more personal like getting married, landing the perfect job, or being able to retire. Steve pointed out that in Philippians 4:10, Paul said he *learned* the secret of contentment. This gives us hope that learning to be content in every situation is a process.

I often get frustrated with my occasional lack of contentment, knowing that I should be content at all times. Sure, God has given us dreams and goals that we are hungry to attain, yet my goal is to feel complete and content even when running after these goals. Contentment is something we all have to work at, but we all can get there. This reminds me of one of my dad's favorite movie quotes. In *Cool Runnings*, just before the Jamaican bobsled team competes in the Olympics, the coach tells the sled driver, "If you aren't good enough without [the gold medal], you will never be good enough with it." Such a good word at just the right time.

Then we went to church and heard something very similar. The pastor spoke about the way Jesus' death and resurrection allows us to live fully in the moment. The veil separating God and man has been torn away, and we have complete access to the presence of God. This is the key to living in the moment and getting the most out of every moment: making sure that we are aware of and walking in the presence of God. This is the abundant life that Jesus was talking about in John 10:10.

Afternoon workout
▶ Easy 70-minute run

Total miles: 9

Ran in Middlesex. Felt weird—kind of low energy, or maybe it was the disruption in my normal daily routine. It might take a bit to clear out all the junk from the big run.

TWO
WEEKS TO BOSTON

MONDAY, APRIL 5

Morning workout
▶ Long run (2 hours)
Total miles: 20.5

Ran from the race start out to the base of Heartbreak Hill. Beautiful day today. Ran smart. With two weeks to go, I need to stop running as hard as I usually do. I was glad I had my Garmin on so I could use it as my governor. I ran the first 90 minutes easy, not allowing myself to run faster than a six-minute pace, and then ran 10 by 90 seconds hard, 90 seconds jog. These miles ended up being a little quicker than six-minute pace, but the effort was far below my usual long-run effort. I could tell I didn't go all that hard because I was wired the rest of the day. Even Sara joked that I must not have run hard enough, which is exactly what I wanted today. It should leave me feeling pretty fresh for next week.

Training for a marathon is the reverse of racing a marathon. You train the first ten weeks with your heart, pouring yourself into every workout, and then you run the last two weeks with your head, purposefully not allowing your heart to take your legs even close to the well. But when you race a marathon, run the first 20 miles with your head, keeping your emotions, excitement, and energy harnessed until the last 10k, when you let everything in your heart out.

TUESDAY, APRIL 6

Morning workout
▶ Easy 45-minute run
Total miles: 6.5

Legs felt good today. Didn't have the fatigue and tightness I usually feel coming out of a long run.

Afternoon workout
▶ Easy 40-minute run
Total miles: 6

Legs felt good. Nice flat bike path called the Minuteman Bikeway. A cyclist stopped me and told me I was the most famous person he had ever seen on the path. Made me laugh!

WEDNESDAY, APRIL 7

Morning workout
▶ 20-minute warm-up with drills and strides
▶ Intervals: 8 by 1k in 2:50 with 90-second rests
▶ 20-minute cooldown
Total miles: 10.5

When I arrived at the train station in Wellesley to pick up Mike,* the temperatures were rising fast. What a beautiful day on the course. I've trained on the course a dozen times or so, but this was the first time I felt a tailwind! It really does exist!

Had a great workout. Legs felt really good. Not hammering Monday's long run left my legs feeling much fresher than they typically do. Ran my

---

* Mike Moffo, my friend and advisor to the Steps Foundation.

intervals between mile 15 on the course to a spot near the bottom of Heartbreak Hill at mile 20. After being on these hills so many times, I think the key is going to be to not overwork the hills. If I am confident enough to relax and run slower up the hills, I could reap a big reward and be able to hammer between the hills and down the backside of Heartbreak on the Graveyard Mile.

INSPIRING RUNNING BOOKS AND MOVIES

My all-time favorite running movie is *Chariots of Fire*. When I was first getting into running, my dad rented it for our Friday movie night. I was quickly asleep. I think it was a year or so before I had the patience to watch it all the way through, but once I was old enough to be content with a good story and not simply action and drama, I was hooked. I watched *Chariots of Fire* before nearly every race in high school.

I also enjoyed both of the Prefontaine movies. However, though these movies were inspiring, they contributed to my stubborn refusal to move up to distances longer than the mile. Like Pre, I wasn't about to let anyone tell me I wasn't fast enough.

I have enjoyed reading many great running books. The Eric Liddell story in *Pure Gold* is a great read. I also enjoyed *The Greatest: The Haile Gebrselassie Story*. Some of his workouts in this book will blow your mind. Other great reads I have enjoyed include *Paula: My Story So Far, In Quest of Gold: The Jim Ryun Story, Born to Run, Run: The Mind-Body Method of Running by Feel*, and the *The 50 Greatest Marathon Races of All Time*.

However, I still feel that the best book for a runner to read is the Bible. The principles of the Bible are designed to set us completely free in every area of life, and that can help us unlock maximum human potential.

My joy and freedom are increasing with every workout. I'm having a great time running. After the workout I met Bill Rogers and did some TV interviews and footage. He is such a laid-back, positive, and friendly guy. I have a huge amount of respect for him, not only because he won Boston and

New York four times apiece, but also because of the way he connects with each of the many fans he has in Boston. I admire him for the joy he exudes.

Bill was asked what it would mean if I won the Boston Marathon. He responded that it would be huge for distance running in America and in the world. I caught myself starting to get nervous as he responded, but I have learned to focus not on things too far down the road, but on the step right in front of me. Dietrich Bonhoeffer wrote about not thinking of the difficult road ahead, but instead focusing on Jesus, who is with us. He wrote, "He leads the way, keep close to Him." Lead on, Jesus!

Afternoon workout
▶ Easy 30-minute run

Total miles: 4

Ran a couple of strides to help Sara with her 300s. Legs felt good this afternoon, but it was hot! I am not used to 85 degrees anymore and feel as if I'm melting. On to a Red Sox vs. Yankees game!

THURSDAY, APRIL 8

Morning workout
▶ Easy 50-minute run

Total miles: 7

Ran on the bike path in Lexington where I am going to do a tempo run on Saturday. Legs felt pretty good.

Sara and I were joking that we are opposites. She starts out fast and feels best at the beginning of easy runs, but I take a good 20 minutes to get my legs loose, and I start feeling good halfway into the run. I guess that's why she's a miler and I'm a marathoner.

Afternoon workout
▶ Easy 25-minute run with drills

Total miles: 3.5

Sara and I did a little exploring in the town of Waltham. Legs felt solid. It's amazing how the high temps can fluctuate from mid eighties one day to low sixties the next. Any weather is possible on marathon day.

FRIDAY, APRIL 9

Morning workout
▶ Easy 50-minute run

Total miles: 7

Ran around Harvard in the cold and rain, but I felt pretty good. I expected to feel like a million bucks with two successive easy days, but that wasn't the case. Tapering is such a weird thing. I never know how I am going to feel. I remember Deena talking about how terrible she felt when tapering, and I can relate sometimes.

Throughout my buildup, I probably assumed I would feel supremely good during my taper and idealized how great I will feel the last week before the marathon. The reality is never quite as sensational as that. Besides, my body and legs go through different cycles when resting. When I begin to rest, I feel great. My body seems to be super responsive to any rest it gets because it normally doesn't get much. But after a week or so of backing off, I start to feel a little sluggish on the easy runs. Still, I know the rest allows me to go deeper to the well on race day. I think strides and drills are critical during the taper phase to help work through some of the sluggishness. Glad I have some scheduled tonight.

Afternoon workout
- 20-minute warm-up with drills
- Intervals: 6 by 200 at 30 seconds with 90 seconds rest
- 10-minute cooldown

Total miles: 4.5

Felt terrible this afternoon. Thirty-second 200s shouldn't be a problem for someone whose job is running, but I was certainly struggling out there this afternoon. I just couldn't lift my knees and had no drive in my legs. Part of it might have been the pesky rain I was running into or the lack of caffeine. Whatever it was, it made it difficult to enjoy the afternoon. It doesn't really matter how the 200s felt—I had the same problem with fast strides before London—but it's still hard not to get rattled when I don't feel good. I tell myself all the right things, but I still fall into a foul mood. I guess I still have some room to grow.

I was still in a bad mood when we went to an International House of Prayer meeting in downtown Boston. Sara is going to have to be patient with me this week. The hardest thing about tapering is keeping my head on straight. I need to spend lots of time praying, reading the Bible, and worshipping God to get to the starting line in the right state of mind.

SATURDAY, APRIL 10

Morning workout
- 20-minute warm-up with drills and strides
- 8-mile tempo run
- 20-minute cooldown

Total miles: 14

It was a windy day out there today, and 4:50s felt much tougher than I hope they will feel on race day. But I guess running a third of the race distance at race pace isn't supposed to feel like a walk in the park. This was my last substantial work at race pace, so I will go into the race feeling humble, which is good. Now I need to stay close, stay low, and stay loving in my attitude toward God. Am I able to run three times this far at this pace? I'm glad I always feel better on race day.

Afternoon workout
▶ Easy 25-minute run

Total miles: 4

I was breathing hard this afternoon. Don't know what the deal is. Coming down from altitude is weird. One day I feel like a million bucks, and the next day I feel as if I'm still at altitude. I guess it's good to anticipate breathing hard in the race. When I come down from altitude, I usually expect the race to feel really easy. Not this year.

SUNDAY, APRIL 11

Morning workout
▶ Easy 60-minute run with drills

Total miles: 8

Now I know I am officially tapering. I woke up at three and lay in bed for an hour or so. Finally I got on my iPhone and read some news, searched for ideas for Sara's birthday on Thursday, and wrote some e-mail interviews. Then I took some melatonin and slept for another hour.

The hardest thing to do on race week is to not overthink things. Sara reminded me of what I always tell her: "Just get to the starting line." At night, I can lay in bed and think myself into a frenzy. Sometimes I'm better off getting up and doing something else to redirect my mind. It may be a long week.

Ran 60 minutes around Walden pond. My legs felt all right, but nothing special. Fun to go on an exploration run in the woods. Reminded me of training in Big Bear before the Olympics.

FAVORITE RUNNERS AND INSPIRING HEROES

My favorite runner is my wife, Sara! In high school, I admired Sara for her amazing running ability. But at the Footlocker National Regional Meet in our junior year, I saw the heart behind the athlete. Sara had been a phenom since she was a freshman in high school (she was the first girl in California to win four state cross-country titles) and was one of the favorites to win the national title. However, at the Western Regional meet she had an uncharacteristically off day, finished tenth, and failed to qualify for the finals. If I were in her shoes, I would have jogged from the finish line straight to the car and been home before the award ceremony began, but not Sara. She had a good cry and then graciously congratulated every one of the girls who qualified for nationals. Sara is truly gracious in victory and defeat, and for this and many other qualities, she is a hero to me.

I grew up admiring Eric Liddell (from the classic running movie *Chariots of Fire*). He was known for his great running passion and deep faith. I didn't know exactly how to integrate my faith and my running, but I knew from Eric's example that it was possible. He gave the world a glimpse of what is possible on the track with God.

I also admired Jim Ryun, the first high-school runner to break four minutes in the mile and an eventual world record holder in the mile. Jim and his family helped me begin to understand how to integrate my faith with running. Between my sophomore and junior years in high school, I stumbled across Jim Ryun Running Camp (which continues today), and I made my first trip across the country to spend a week in Wichita, Kansas.

At this point, Jim Ryun was already my hero. I had watched *Jim Ryun: America's Greatest Miler* at least a hundred times. I could practically recite it. One day, Jim called my house, and my mom told him I was watching the video. He replied, "Tell him to read his Bible instead." Not the response I was expecting.

Going to the running camp changed my life. I instantly became a part of the Ryun family and began learning about how running should flow out of my faith, not the other way around. I began to build my own faith at camp that year. Jim is one of my heroes because he is up-front about where his talent came from and how faith helped him handle the many highs and lows of his career. Today, he continues to use his running fame as a powerful way to help other people.

Jim's son Drew lived with my family and trained in Big Bear for three months during my senior year. Drew introduced me to Stanford and to Sara, and he continues to be a major influencer in my life. I am blessed to call Drew, Jim, and all the Ryun family not only heroes but also friends.

My father is also a big hero to me. He knew before I did that God had given me the talent to compete with the best runners in the world, yet he never forced me to run. I am deeply thankful for this. If my dad had forced me to run, I would have never made it through all those tough moments when the only motivation that worked came from a seed God planted deep within me. I was blessed to grow up with a very encouraging family. Mom's and Dad's unwavering belief in me gave me the foundation I needed to become the person I am today. I hope that I can do the same for my own kids someday.

Week Fourteen

ONE
WEEK TO BOSTON

MONDAY, APRIL 12

Morning workout
▶ Easy run (1 hour, 30 minutes)
Total miles: 14.65

Had fun running from the Marathon start to about the Whole Foods in Newton. It was a beautiful day on the course. Legs felt good. I decided not to look at my watch the whole way so I wouldn't be concerned with pace. Afterward, I was surprised that I averaged nearly six-minute pace with so little effort. I really have a good grasp of the course now. I know what lies ahead, and I'm familiar with the atmosphere around me and feel comfortable in it. That's so important. No more runs on the course. Rest mode shifts up a gear today.

Before the run this morning, Sara and I had a great time of talking and praying. I come away from those experiences feeling much lighter in spirit. I'm surprised that I don't realize that I'm carrying around a heaviness of spirit until it's lifted through times of prayer like this. Sara reminded me of the time I encouraged her to run as if she couldn't fail. As soon as she repeated those words to me, I knew they were exactly what I needed to hear.

I so easily get focused on the way I am feeling, the perfect race strategy, and the need to execute it perfectly. I start wondering if I'm making a tower of cards and if the slightest wrong move could send the whole thing top-pling down. That's not freedom. That's not running as if I can't fail—it's just trying not to mess up. I have watched a lot of great football and basketball teams suffer upsets after getting a comfortable lead and going into a prevent defense rather than staying on the offensive. Trying not to mess up is no way to perform or to live. It's not the freedom that Christ came to gave us. By faith I am going to run a week from today with this freedom. I will run as if I can't fail.

I need to continue to practice an unrelenting trust in God's goodness. I know that God is a good God. Good things might not always happen to me or around me, but I know I can trust that God is always good, His grace is always sufficient, and He is all I need to have the best life possible. A lot of my worry, anxiety, and uncertainty about the future comes from not fully trusting my heavenly Father. If I fully trust Him, I can let go of all my burdens and just run with joy, and that is my heart's deepest desire for this race. The joy of the Lord is my strength.

TUESDAY, APRIL 13

Morning workout
▶ Easy 40-minute run
Total miles: 6

Legs felt good running around Harvard this morning. Another beautiful day here in Boston. I've been checking the weather frequently. Race day is looking good so far. Mostly sunny, highs in the upper fifties with lows in the forties. The real element to look at is the wind.

Busy but fun day planned today. E-mail interviews, phone interviews, and a trip to a local homeless shelter to present a check from the Hall Steps Foundation to Back On My Feet, an organization that works with the homeless to help them get out of homelessness through a running program. It gives these people not only practical training in life skills but also a goal to train for, which increases their sense of purpose. I am excited to give back to the cities like Boston that provide me with such an incredible platform on which to compete.

Afternoon workout
▶ Easy 25-minute run

Total miles: 3.5

Legs felt all right today. Had an "only in Boston" encounter—a car pulled up next to me, and I expected the driver to ask for directions or something. Instead, she asked for an autograph. I felt humbled, but I was also protective of my time to just enjoy my run, so I politely declined. I felt kind of bad afterward, but I was in the middle of a run and she was in the middle of traffic, so I'm not sure how it would have worked out.

One of the things about having any level of prominence is figuring out how to balance all the other things that come with the job. Should I have stopped in the middle of my run to sign the autograph? My runs are my personal times, and I enjoy having scheduled appearances for pictures and autographs. I can see how famous athletes and celebrities get a bad rap for declining interviews, autographs, and pictures. After all, the reporter or autograph seeker is just one person, and how long could one autograph or interview take? But the athlete may have just signed autographs for an hour and may be tired, hungry, and ready to rest. If they stop to sign one autograph, one could turn into ten or a hundred. I know this isn't always the case, and some celebrities are not as receptive to fans as they should be, but I think we all need to extend more grace to everyone, including celebrities.

Went to a Hillsong concert tonight. Hillsong has always been a powerful worship band for me to listen to. The presence of God is thick when they play—I can feel it. When I listen to their music and picture myself running to it, I can see myself running with God and with the heart He wants me to have. That's why I have put many of my workout videos to their music.

At the concert, I felt encouraged to run with untouchable joy. I pictured myself living as joyfully as if I had just run the race of my life. I felt God's presence and the joy that it brings, just as I know I will feel them during the race. It is the sweetest sensation—something was unlocked in my spirit that will empower me to run with the joy of the Lord. I will indeed laugh because of the goodness of God as I run down Boylston. God is so good!

WEDNESDAY, APRIL 14

Morning workout
▶ 20-minute warm-up with drills and strides
▶ Intervals: 4 by 1 mile with 2 minutes rest in 4:40, 4:45, 4:30, 4:35
▶ 4-minute rest and one 800 in 2:12
▶ 20-minute cooldown

Total miles: 10

Legs felt good today. Had a good workout. Good to end all the hard workouts on a positive note. A 4:50 pace still doesn't feel easy, but I feel strong, and I know that with God all things are possible.

I usually try to air it out on the last rep of this particular workout, but I didn't feel the need to do that this time around. I just need to rest and let my legs come to full life, so I ran slower than I was supposed to, and it felt right.

Afternoon workout
▶ Easy 20-minute run

Total miles: 3

Legs felt good this afternoon. Lots of rest and lots of fuel. This week it's important to err on the side of being overly fueled. I'd rather have 1000 calories too many than 200 calories not enough.

THURSDAY, APRIL 15

Morning workout
▶ Easy 50-minute run

Total miles: 8

Happy birthday, Sara! Glad she didn't have to drive six hours to L.A. and stand in a long line to get our taxes in the mail at the last minute like she did last year. We have some fun stuff planned for today, including dinner with her sister at a great Jamaica Plain restaurant and a Blue Man Group show.

Ran on the Minuteman Bikeway. Last run before moving into our hotel in the big city with all the Marathon buzz in full effect. This is when it starts to get exciting. It's the one weekend of the year when I feel like a rock star. The fans here are incredibly knowledgeable and enthusiastic about running.

God's presence was thick in my Bible study with Sara this morning. Psalm 2:4, "He who sits in the heavens laughs," spoke to my spirit in such a strong way. During this entire buildup, I've sensed God telling me that I will laugh coming down Boylston Street. I have seen myself over and over again running down Boylston, completely satisfied with God and His goodness and with what He has done in my life and in this race. I can see it so strongly. I keep thinking about the Hillsong concert, where I was encouraged that God will enable me to live as joyfully (regardless of the race results) as I would if I had just broken the world record and won Olympic gold all in one race.

Psalm 2:4 is the key. Because I am seated in heaven, I can laugh in any circumstance. God has "seated us with Him in the heavenly places in Christ Jesus."* It is kind of a trippy thing to think about, and I can't fully grasp it, but maintaining the perspective that I am in heaven right now changes everything. The view from heaven is a lot different from the way I normally see things. I get worried and anxious about a lot of stuff, but with a heavenly perspective, I see the big picture. "Set your mind on the things above, not on the things that are on earth."† Having a heavenly perspective is a huge part of unlocking freedom and joy in everything—especially in things that I care a lot about and am invested in.

FRIDAY, APRIL 16

Morning workout
▶ Easy 20-minute run

Total miles: 3

Legs felt good this morning. The special feeling that runners hope will

---

* Ephesians 2:6

† Colossians 3:2

come with a taper is starting to come on. Legs feel light and full of run. The weather is cold and rainy. The forecast is looking good for the race— a high of 55 and a low of 45 with some cloud cover. Press conference this morning.

Afternoon workout
- 20-minute warm-up with drills and strides
- 2-mile tempo run in 10 minutes
- Intervals: 4 by 400 with 90 seconds rest in 66
- 20-minute cooldown

Total miles: 9

Legs felt good today. Five-minute pace still doesn't feel like a jog, but running fast never feels like a jog. The key is having the strength to handle the pace. I'm excited that my heart is right and that I have the right perspective.

At the press conference today, I was asked repeatedly about last year's race, what I learned from last year, about Meb winning the most recent NYC Marathon, and about what I learned from the NYC Marathon. I realized that I didn't have the best perspective going into NYC. Workouts had gone so well and I felt so fit that I was expecting it to feel easy. I had very high expectations. Building up to this race, I may not have knocked any workouts out of the park, but I am humble and ready for a battle. I am walking by faith—no workouts have been floating effortlessly, but my trust is in God. But most important, I am after the joy of the Lord more than the title.

SATURDAY, APRIL 17

Morning workout
- Easy 40-minute run with drills and strides

Total miles: 6

Legs felt okay, but not great. Today was a long day. It started with a couple hours of restless sleep last night. I couldn't help thinking about the race and was starting to feel a little anxious, but I was able to battle it off and go back to sleep, trusting in God's goodness and convinced that He is enough. The last two days are always difficult. I have gotten better at remaining confident, but I always have to battle doubts.

A lot of laying around today. Sara's race is tomorrow, so we hardly left the hotel after getting back from our run. We ordered take-out, got therapy in the hotel, and visited with family in our room.

SUNDAY, APRIL 18

Morning workout
▶ Easy 35-minute run with drills and strides

Total miles: 7

Legs felt great today. Once again, I'm amazed by the difference a day can make. Was it the therapy I got? Or the beginning of my carbohydrate loading yesterday? Or the excitement of the race? Whatever it was, I felt a hundred times better than yesterday, and best of all, I could sense God's peace in a really strong way. "You will keep him in perfect peace, whose mind is stayed on You, because he trusts in You."* As I trust more and more in God, I will experience more and more peace in everything I do. God is so good, and He really is all I need. If tomorrow doesn't result in a victory, I am steadfast in knowing that God is still good and life is still beautiful. Tomorrow will be fun, and the joy of the Lord will pour out of me. That's all I could hope for. God's goodness transcends my circumstances.

MONDAY, APRIL 19: MARATHON DAY

At nine last night, I set my alarm for six and went to bed. I woke up this morning at five thirty after a crazy dream.

In the dream, Sara, my brother Chad, and I were staying out in Waltham. I woke up on marathon day and noticed right away that it was oddly bright

---

* Isaiah 26:3 NKJV

outside. I quickly glanced at my bedside clock, which read eight fifteen—I had missed the bus to the start by more than an hour, and the start of the race was less than two hours away. I quickly threw down my prerace breakfast of sourdough bread, olive oil, and Muscle Milk while yelling at Chad to hurry up and get in the car. But then my eyes suddenly flashed open, and I was glad to see only a dim morning light.

Marathon day. I had been praying about this day since I decided to run Boston for the first time more than two years ago.

I found my phone and tried to not wake Sara. She had taken the brunt of my last few restless nights. Fortunately, last night was much better. I found my water bottle and put down the 20 ounces of water I drink first thing every morning. My iPhone showed the current temperature was 42 with a light wind out of the northwest—a tailwind. Perfect.

My stealth mode wasn't very effective, and Sara began stirring as I ate the first half of my breakfast. I finished dressing for the race just before Coach arrived to pick up my hydration bottles, which race workers would set up on tables every 5k on the course.

I am always amazed by all the preparation for a marathon. Last night I made sure to charge my iPod Shuffle and my Garmin 110. Then I make sure I have toilet paper (in case the Port-a-Potties run out, as they often do before races), a gel to take after my warm-up, spot Band-Aids to protect from nipple rash, arm warmers and beanies, gum to keep from getting parched at the starting line, extra socks in case my feet get wet on the warm-up, compression socks in case the temperature drops below 40 degrees, Cytomax performance beverage to sip before the race, my iPhone so I can read the Bible on the bus ride and check the weather before leaving for the start, my Oakley sunglasses with different lens options, racing flats, a singlet, gloves, and plenty of water.

At six thirty we headed down to the lobby to meet my agent, who was nervous because we were late (it runs in the Hall family), and leave for the John Hancock Center to catch the bus, which was scheduled to depart at seven. I wasn't my typical nervous self this morning. In previous marathons, I felt as if I was heading into a battle from which I was not likely to return (similar to the mind-set the runners had in the first running of the Boston Marathon). With the emotional goodbyes and well-wishing, not getting emotional is usually a challenge, but this morning I felt very calm and relaxed.

The volunteers at the John Hancock Center formed a cheering tunnel for all us elite athletes to walk through on our way to the bus. Sara had been quickly throwing all our stuff in bags so we could check out of our hotel room after the race, so she rejoined me at the bus. Having Sara accompany me to the start was a blessing and helped to keep my nerves at bay. I still had three long hours to wait before the gun.

I knew this year's Boston Marathon would be a memorable one because the organizers brought in many of the best marathoners in the world. Last year, when I finished third here, I had come into the run with the fastest personal best in the field. But this year, ten of us had personal bests under 2:08. Abderrahim Goumri of Morocco had a personal best of 2:05. Deriba Merga of Ethiopia was the defending Boston champion and finished fourth at the 2008 Olympics. My teammate and friend Meb was fresh off his NYC Marathon win. And a whole bunch of other Kenyan and Ethiopian athletes also had impressive credentials. With that many quality runners, I really didn't know who the biggest challenge would come from.

On marathon day, a guy who slips in under the radar could have a breakthrough day. The marathon is very hit-or-miss, which is why those few athletes who are able to win time and time again are so impressive. But even the most consistent runners have off days. I was running with Haile Gebrselassie at the 15-mile mark of the 2007 London Marathon when he dropped out. He set a world record in his next marathon and another a year later. History in the marathon means only what we let it mean. Every race day is a fresh opportunity to do something special. Maybe today would be my day.

My mellow mood continued on the bus as I read a couple Bible passages on my iPhone. The passages of the day were from Leviticus and Psalms. The Leviticus passage was about keeping the Sabbath holy and a day of rest. In Psalms, I read David's encouraging words about the goodness of trusting in God. What a great word for today.

The bus ride to Hopkington takes nearly an hour. By the time we arrived, I had finished the second half of my breakfast (I learned from Dr. Clyde to eat the first half when I get up and then wait 45 minutes before eating the second half to keep my blood sugar from spiking). We made our way into a church that is just steps away from the starting line. This is where the elite athletes and other VIPs are held before the race. Sara and I sat and chatted aimlessly with my coach, and then he gave me some race pointers. Work the course the way I did in practice. Don't respond to every crazy move other runners make. The best advice Coach has ever given me is to just be me when I run, which I always think of when I'm on the starting line.

Seventy-five minutes till the gun. I must have checked my watch a hundred times in the next 30 minutes before I began my warm-up. I was eager to get the show on the road after months of buildup and weeks of rest. I sensed God inviting me to fully trust in Him and to let the joy of that trust flow out of me.

Sara and I jogged for 15 minutes on a 200-meter section of the road that was specially taped off for the elite athletes to warm up on. I felt like a horse that was being warmed up on one of those merry-go-round style horse walkers. All of us were nervously eyeing each other. I felt peaceful warming up. I was loose, my legs felt great, and my spirit was light. Sara and I joked with each other about this and that. It was a beautiful day with perfect weather and great opportunity.

Is race day really so different and so much grander than any other day? I try not to make too much out of any one day because life is beautiful every day and should be celebrated. Still, certain days hold unique opportunities or mark the beginning or end of a journey or mission. I am certain Jesus made the most of every day, but I suspect that when He rose on the morning He was to be crucified, He felt that day was a special day. I had a similar feeling that today was one of my special days.

As we jogged past the fired-up masses from the church to the starting line, I fed off their enthusiasm and energy. I high-fived as many runners as I could and yelled into the crowd. I felt as if I were about to lead an invasion of Boston.

At ten, the gun finally released us down one of the steepest hills on the course. In championship-style races (where there are no pacers), everyone looks around during the first 100 meters, feeling each other out to see who is going to take the lead. Another runner jumped into the lead initially, but it was short-lived. After the first 400, I found myself in the lead. I felt much more comfortable and full of peace leading than I did in 2009. Last year, I felt as if I was pushing too hard and trying to force something to happen, but this year, my stride felt smooth, easy, and free-flowing.

I was very relaxed and felt like I was where I was supposed to be, even after I ran by a spectator on the side of the road who cheered for me but then added, "But don't lead the whole way!" I just laughed to myself and continued to run the way I knew God wanted me to run. During that first mile I prayed to God that everyone on the course would encounter Him. I told Him that I knew He is a good Dad and that I trusted in Him regardless of what happened.

I passed through the first mile in 4:52—14 seconds slower than a year ago. Perfect. I could feel the peace of God all around me as a soothing breeze blew my hair to the right. (After the race, Meb told reporters that he was looking at my hair to see which way the wind was blowing.) The pack of mainly African runners seemed content to sit behind and follow my lead.

The pace felt much more comfortable than it did a few weeks earlier on my three by five-mile workout, but the thought still crept into my mind that this would be hard to maintain for 26 miles. However, having gone out much faster at the London marathon in 2008, when I ran 2:06, I knew that sometimes our bodies can do things we cannot wrap our minds around. This is when overthinking can really hurt performance. I put the thought out of my mind and told myself to be in the moment and think only about the present.

I continued leading through Ashland (the two-mile mark) and Framingham (the 10k mark) right on the pace I hoped for: 4:50 per mile. Why have I always loved to lead? Is it because I ran alone so often during my high-school days in Big Bear? Or do I like to control the rhythm of the run? Race announcers and many runners are often critical of leading because breaking the wind takes more energy. I have heard that leading requires 10 percent more energy than following, which might be true, especially on windy days. But the benefits of leading are rarely talked about and are often overlooked. Leading allows you to dictate the pace. Even if the pack is running consistent mile splits, subtle changes of pace constantly occur. At London 2008, we had pacers and ran a consistent 4:46 pace for the first half of the race, but the beginning of every mile felt like a sprint. The race felt uneven because I wasn't dictating the pace. The leader can run exactly the way he feels like running at every moment. Doing this over the distance of a marathon could have a huge positive impact on optimizing results.

Also, something can be said about the excitement of leading a race. I always get most excited when I am engaged up in the front of a race. I realize that everyone is different. Sara certainly doesn't get the same excitement from leading a race until she hits the front in her final kick. Runners need the freedom to find what works for them and race accordingly.

Many people have tried to tell me how to race. I am usually pretty good about sticking to being me, but after a while it can wear on me and start to influence the way I run. For example, before the NYC Marathon, I heard over and over again from the press and others that I should sit back and stay out of the lead. I decided to try it for at least the opening miles. I sat back most of the race—and was dropped at 15 miles. It felt terribly wrong for me to sit back.

Around the nine-mile mark, I relinquished the lead as Merga made the first hard move. He took off as if he were running an all-out mile. I knew we were running plenty fast already and decided to keep the same cadence and pace. When someone makes a move and I don't cover it, either by choice or because I am not physically able, I usually get slightly frustrated. Not today. I felt confident and even a bit peaceful about sitting back and allowing a gap to open. I knew it was the right decision. The pace always slows down after a surge, so I chose to stay reasonably close and then work my way back up when the pace settled. I did this in both my marathons in London, which gave me a lot of confidence that I could do the same here today. Another European runner and I stayed together as we approached ten miles. This was the first time I noticed the wind being a bit pesky. The day had started with what I thought would be a direct tailwind, but when we got to the start in Hopkington, the American flag at the starting line was blowing across us and almost into our faces. Having trained with this same wind for three weeks, I knew that I would feel it at times on the course but that it wouldn't be as bad as last year.

The leaders, including Meb, had a good gap on us as we hit 10 miles— perhaps 20 seconds or so. I gradually dropped the European runner and began working on picking off the runners who were falling off the lead pack. At mile 11, the lead runners began looking around as if to find a designated leader, and I made up ground quickly. As we approached the 20k mark, the leaders were on the left side of the road. I passed them on the right, and they quickly crossed the road and tucked in behind me.

The depth of the marathon has really changed. We were almost halfway through the race and on pace to run 2:06, and 12 guys were still in contention. Not very long ago, only a few runners would ever go out that hard. Our sport and what we elites think is possible at the marathon distance is drastically changing.

Hitting the lead again felt good. I felt a surge of energy but tempered myself from running too hard. In hindsight, I was probably a little too concerned with my splits and should have been more aggressive when I hit highs like I was experiencing. When runners feel a lot of energy but don't use it, they can't always save it for later. Sometimes the highs won't come back, so the best thing to do is to use the energy from them.

I stayed on the right side of the road so I could hear the notorious screaming girls of Wellesley at maximum volume. I was also aware of the tight pack of runners behind me. A lot of moves happen at exciting points on the course. Last year the race broke open at Wellesley, so I was surprised this year when the others were content to sit behind me.

Boy, did I enjoy the crowds at Wellesley! I was feeling their enthusiasm. Running so close to the crowd that some reached out and touched me, I cupped my hand behind my ears as if to say, "I can't hear you!" They released a scream that must have reached heaven. That was one of my fastest and easiest miles of the day. Running this section of the course is indescribable.

I continued to lead through the halfway mark. Our split was 63:27 (4:50 pace)—perfect. I thought to myself that this is exactly where I wanted to be. My effort level felt good, I was excited, and I was leading. I was looking forward to the second half.

This is the spot in the marathon where the difference between paced races and unpaced races is huge. In a paced race, we probably would have come through halfway at about the same split but with much less mental effort and much less surging. Instead of exerting mental energy keeping track of what other runners were doing, we would simply have been staring at the backs of our pacers and trying to conserve as much energy as possible. There would have been no moves in the race up to this point. We would have all been sitting in the pack, zoning out, trying to get to halfway with as much energy as possible still in the tank.

Now, on the other hand, we had spent the last hour looking around at each other and trying to figure who was going to do what, which moves were significant, and so on. I felt as if the race had been going already for an hour, whereas in a paced race, I feel as if the race doesn't start until the rabbit drops out (sometimes not until the 20-mile mark).

At about mile 14, Merga made another move. This one was not as hard as the first. *Good*, I thought to myself. I had taken some of the zip out of his legs already. I had beat him in London '08. Three months later he faded to a dramatic fourth-place finish in the Olympics, where I finished tenth. At Boston '09, he made a hard move at Wellesley and beat four-time Boston champion Robert Cheruiyot, and I finished third.*

The rest of the pack took off after him. Again, we were running plenty fast, and I thought that if I could maintain the 4:50 pace I was currently running, I would win the race. I would never have guessed my calculations were wrong. In hindsight I think I should have made a little move and kept the leaders closer so that when the pace slowed, I wouldn't have so much ground to make up.

By the time we passed the Whole Foods in Newton, where I had begun my interval training sessions leading up to the race, the leaders had a

---

* Cheruiyot didn't compete in this year's race because of an injury.

substantial lead, and I was beginning to feel fatigued. We passed the 14-mile mark and dropped downhill. Just after the 15-mile mark, we hit the first significant long uphill of the race, and I began dealing with a flood of negative thoughts. I quickly reminded myself of my goals for the race: to connect with God, to run free of any burdens others might put on me or I might put on myself, to let out the joy that comes from fully trusting that God is a good Father and knowing that He knows what is best for me and wants to give me just that.

My mind also went back to the hill runs in Mammoth. *Don't focus on knee drive; just turn it over*, I told myself. *Stay relaxed. You're doing great.* It never hurts to remind myself that I am running well when the pack is pulling away. In London 2008, after passing through the halfway mark at what was nearly a world-record pace at the time, I dropped to fifth place. Running alone, I reminded myself that I had a great one going and urged myself to keep pouring it out. I had to feed myself positive encouragement to get through those last hard ten miles.

Running downhill toward the fire station that marks mile 17.5 and the start of the hills of Newton, I watched Meb separate from the lead pack and go to the opposite side of the road. He told me later that he was waving at me to catch up because the pace was slowing and the other guys in the lead pack were missing the tangents. I was about 30 seconds back at the time, which is too much time to make up in one slow mile. Still, I was gaining as the leaders made the turn at the fire station and started up the historic hills at Newton. At this point I was just inside the top ten, but I could see other runners starting to fall off. I was glad to see that Meb wasn't among the casualties.

As I turned the corner, unlike last year, I knew exactly what lay ahead. I recognized the sign that marked the false top of the first hill, which is approximately a third of a mile long. I knew I would go down and then have to come slightly back up before a mile break before the next hill, on which I would pass the 18-mile mark. I remembered Bill Rogers saying he managed his energy on the hills so he was fresh enough to fly down the backside. I told myself not to redline it so I could have my legs under me for the Graveyard Mile.

After the first hill, I still felt okay and was able to get my turnover back for the fast mile between the first and second hill. When I got to the light that marked the start of the second hill, I knew that I would have less space to recover before hitting Heartbreak Hill. Coming up the second hill was very difficult, but I was blessed with great crowd support pulling me up the hill, including the Bentley track team chanting my name as I ran by. We had met them a week earlier on their track, which was only a few miles from where we were staying in Waltham. It's always encouraging to see familiar faces in painful moments.

Heartbreak Hill isn't the worst of the three hills, but it comes at the end of a tough three-mile stretch of the road at a difficult point in any marathon. When I saw the familiar shops come into view, I knew Heartbreak was coming, and I took a deep breath and prepared for the final ascent. After this hill I would get a nice downhill mile to recover and get my turnover back. I continued to remind myself to run with joy.

By the time I was headed down the Graveyard Mile, I was in sixth place. A Kenyan runner was coming back to me, and unfortunately, Meb was no longer with the leaders and wasn't that far off in the distance. I knew at this point in the race, with the amount of fatigue in my legs, I would have to use the course to generate speed. One of the best pieces of running advice I have ever gotten is to consciously put five or ten quick steps together at the top of all hills and after all sharp corners as a way to get back up to speed quickly. My legs still felt reasonably good at this point, so I was able to manage some decent splits coming down the hill.

The most rowdy (though not necessarily the loudest) crowd on the course is at Boston College. There, the crowd is deep, the kids have a good time, and I feel as if I'm running through a festival. The students' enthusiasm gets me going for the difficult last four miles.

Turning the corner onto Beacon Street, I passed the Kenyan runner. I was wondering what was going on up front. I could see Meb but not the other three guys in front of him. I looked up and was disappointed to see the helicopter tracking the lead runner. It was a long way off, so unless a catastrophe occurred up front, this would not be the day I would win the Boston Marathon.

I briefly thought to myself about all my family and friends who had good feelings about this race, and about all the encouragement I had received. Having a vision gives me hope and direction, but it doesn't come prepackaged with a guarantee when it will be fulfilled. I have a vision of running supernaturally, just as Elijah did when he outran a chariot to Jezreel, but I have yet to experience it. Does that mean the vision isn't valid? No, a vision like this doesn't foretell the future; it reveals our potential when we partner with God. The challenge is to believe and to act accordingly. True belief changes our actions. Discovering our God-given potential unlocks tremendous power. This knowledge gives us hope as we look into the future.

Visions often leave out other specific details as well. Supernatural running might not be running a world record. It might be running with supernatural joy despite having an off day, or running for something more than times and medals—something like running in order to impact the lives of the poor all over the world.

My heart was pounding, and I was fighting the temptation to settle for where I was at. I was in fifth place and on pace to run a solid time. Catching the leaders seemed unlikely, so why push my body through those last few extremely painful miles? Meb's white jersey wasn't urging me on. Even if Meb hadn't been my friend, I wouldn't have been hugely motivated to beat him. I had teammates in college who were fired up about beating other guys. That's what drove them. I have never found that kind of competitiveness all that motivating, healthy, or fun. I can push myself further by competing with a heart of love, joy, and praise to God. I have a hard time imagining Jesus being driven to beat someone. Jesus ran His own race and accomplished the unique goal that God set before Him so we should do the same.

In those last few miles, I ran with pure joy—not because I was feeling so great or the race was coming easily (on the contrary, my whole body hurt), but because I was running the race set before me. I knew my Father was proud of me, and I reveled in His goodness.

Around mile 24 I passed Meb. I wanted to encourage him but wasn't able to do anything but put my hand on his bald head as a gesture of support and compassion. I kept telling myself to turn it over as fast as I could. The

Citgo sign marking the final mile was a welcome sight. The crowd was as loud as ever, and I poured myself into the last mile. I told myself to pour out everything I had until I got to Boylston Street, where I could let out whatever joy was in me in the form of celebration. I had been looking forward to turning onto Boylston for months, so I wasn't going to let the moment pass without celebrating it.

Reflecting on the last mile, I'm reminded of a childhood memory. On family outings to cut firewood, my dad ran the chainsaw, and my brothers and I carried the wood to the truck. We turned the chore into a game, challenging ourselves to see how much wood we could carry all the way to the truck. We stacked wood so high in each other's arms, we couldn't see anything in front of us. Even when we weren't sure we could manage any more wood, we would say, "One more."

I learned a lot from those experiences. I learned to not think about the distance to the truck, to clear my mind, and then to think only about the next step in front of me. I also learned that my body was usually capable of carrying more wood than I thought it could handle. Pushing yourself to the brink is an acquired skill. It develops with time and practice and takes self-confidence and the boldness to test the body's limit.

I also had to learn to deal with failure. I didn't make it to the truck every time. Sometimes, one more piece was more than I could carry, and I had to learn to deal with that reality without losing hope and confidence in myself. I learned to not get rattled by failure. I also learned the amazing feeling of arriving at my destination having achieved my goal. The sense of accomplishment was profound. In those final steps, my arms would be red and shaking as the sharp bark and twigs pierced my skin, but I learned to ignore the pain and focus on putting one step in front of the other. I learned the joy of testing my boundaries.

This is the same joy that comes out in the final miles of a marathon. When I hit the final stretch of Boylston, having tested my boundaries, I let my joy out. With my arms spread wide, I "airplaned," weaving from side to side across the road. I hadn't had this kind of joy at the end of race since my amazing spiritual experience of winning the 2008 U.S. Olympic Marathon Trials. I was in mid-flight when I noticed one of the thousands of fans lining the street going crazy, yelling at me, "You can get Merga!" My eyes popped up and I could see Merga's yellow jersey 100 meters in front of me.

With only 600 meters to go, I had serious doubts that I could catch him and finish on the podium, but I decided to forgo my celebration until after the finish line and started pumping my arms as hard as I could. (My legs had ceased to respond to any mental urgings miles ago.) I felt as if I were in my recurring dream of running a race and feeling as if I'm caught in quicksand. But Merga's figure was getting closer. As I neared the grandstands, the decibel level of the crowd grew louder still, and for a minute I thought I might be able to sneak by Mergo and onto the podium. But Merga heard the crowd roar, realized what was happening, checked how much distance he had, and put in a mini-surge. I finished just two seconds out of third place, but that didn't really matter. I had won—I had found joy!

TUESDAY, APRIL 20

Morning workout

▶ Very easy 50-minute run

Total miles: 6

My last run for two weeks. There was something strangely beautiful about today's run. The bright blue sun-filled sky warmed me as I jogged next to Sara, Kathy, and Kelly, friends who developed our Steps Foundation website. Something in my spirit smiled. I sometimes experience a postrace letdown after a marathon, but not this day. It was as if I had continued right on through the finish of yesterday's race and kept running in the same spirit of joy I had experienced so powerfully yesterday. As I ran through the cherry blossoms on Beacon Street, where I had sprinted just 24 hours earlier, my joy was untouchable. It wasn't wrapped around winning a race, setting a personal best, or any other outcome. It was an inner joy that cannot be shaken or taken from me. The funny thing is that when the spirit is filled with joy, the body is too. My legs certainly didn't feel great when I started jogging, but by the end of the run, I felt the urge to open up and run one last mile. Of course, I didn't. I bottled the feeling, knowing that the end of one journey is only the beginning of another.

LIST OF SIDEBARS

The Mammoth Track Club 13
Training to Race vs. Training to Get Fit 32
Heart Rate Monitors and Aerobic Threshold 35
Alternating Fast and Slow Days 47
Hills and Flats 51
Short and Long Runs 57
Training at Altitude 61
Trails, Tracks, and Pavement 69
Training in All Seasons 72
Weekly Mileage 79
Rest 83
Tapering Training into Races 92
Recovering After Races 95
Stretching 103
Cross Training 108
Injuries 115
Blisters 126
Shoes 134
Clothing 139
Energy Food 145
Electrolyte Replacement Drinks 149
Hydration Systems 156
All About Equipment 161
Running in Groups and Running Alone 168
Running Logs 171
Inspiring Running Books and Movies 179
Favorite Runners and Inspiring Heroes 184